Bhagavan Sri
Sathya Sai Baba
My Divine Teacher

Bhagavan Sri
SATHYA SAI BABA
MY DIVINE TEACHER

Curth Orefjaerd

MOTILAL BANARSIDASS PUBLISHERS
PRIVATE LIMITED • DELHI

First Indian Edition: Delhi, 1994
Reprint: Delhi, 1995

Translated from Swedish by Sisko Orefjaerd
Edited by Ian Abrahams, Sydney, Australia
Proof-reading by Bernard Gow, Sydney, Australia

ISBN: 81-208-1269-1 (Cloth)
ISBN: 81-208-1270-5 (Paper)

Also available at:
MOTILAL BANARSIDASS
41 U.A. Bungalow Road, Jawahar Nagar, Delhi 110 007
120 Royapettah High Road, Mylapore, Madras 600 004
16 St. Mark's Road, Bangalore 560 001
Ashok Rajpath, Patna 800 004
Chowk, Varanasi 221 001

PRINTED IN INDIA
BY JAINENDRA PRAKASH JAIN AT SHRI JAINENDRA PRESS,
A-45 NARAINA, PHASE I, NEW DELHI 110 028
AND PUBLISHED BY NARENDRA PRAKASH JAIN FOR
MOTILAL BANARSIDASS PUBLISHERS PRIVATE LIMITED,
BUNGALOW ROAD, DELHI 110 007

Curth Orefjaerd

In deep love and humble gratitude I lay this work at the Divine Lotus Feet of my beloved Teacher—
Bhagavan Sri Sathya Sai Baba

Acknowledgements

I wish to convey my sincere, heartfelt gratitude to all dear friends in India, the USA, Australia and in Sweden who have supported and encouraged me to fulfil this work.

Special heartfelt thanks I owe to my dear wife, Sisko, for her patient assistance and translation of the original Swedish version into English. Also to Ian Abrahams and Bernard Gow for transforming the text into grammatically correct English as well as their invaluable help with administration of the manuscript to the book you now hold.

Likewise my warm thanks to Richard LeVan for his wholehearted engagement and help with much valuable advice.

A special thanks and gratitude goes to Howard Murphet, whose first book, "Sai Baba, Man Of Miracles," paved the way for me to come to the Feet of the Avatar, and who kindly accepted to write the foreword.

Foreword

I feel it is a privilege to write a foreword for this book because of the spiritual quality of its content. Perhaps I was invited to perform this task because I was instrumental in introducing the author to Sri Sathya Sai Baba. In the earlier part of this volume the author states that it was my book, "Sai Baba, Man Of Miracles," that turned his searching footsteps hurrying towards Puttaparthi.

Sai Baba has said on several occasions that He calls only those who are ready to come to Him. But, He adds, that there are different levels of readiness. The fact that Curth Orefjaerd writes that Sai Baba spoke to him from every page of my modest volume, suggests that he must have been in an advanced state of readiness. I know of course that I was no more than the instrumental hand opening a window in the wall of maya through which the Divine Voice could be heard calling the Swedish searcher to the place of great peace and true learning.

But, when on the day of his arrival, Curth first sat on the sand in front of the Mandir at Prasanthi Nilayam and saw the red robe moving towards him, he felt so overwhelmed, so near to being completely undone, that inwardly he prayed to Sai Baba that He would come no closer. Just then, Baba, who reads all hearts, understood the Swede's inner state and promptly veered away to give His attention to other people sitting in the line for darshan.

It reminds me of the scene in the Bhagavad Gita where Arjuna was shown the true Divine Form of Lord Krishna. He was so overcome by the experience that he begged Krishna to return promptly to His human form. Likewise, when Moses asked to see the God who was speaking to him on the mountain top, he was told that he would not be able to bear such a sight and was shown only the back of the Almighty One as He moved away.

In the same manner Sai Baba compassionately showed only His back to the sensitive Swede, realising that at that moment Curth's vision of the Divine within the human Sai form would be more than he could sustain with equanimity. Later on, however, when the author had gained control of his deep inner reactions, Swami took him into the Mandir and proceeded to give him a series of wonderful experiences. These experiences over a long period with the insights he gained from them, the author shares with his readers in the pages of this volume. Some devotees at the ashram asked, and some of the readers may ask, why Curth received such special treatment, such amazing grace from the Avatar. But the humble Swede could only reply that he did not know why.

The fact is that the omniscient avataric Teacher treats every individual according to his or her capacity to receive; each according to his or her needs and level of progress along the path of return. What is appropriate for one is not for another. The Lord knows whether the most effective stimulus should be divine nectar or unpleasant medicine with or without a spoonful of sugar.

It was not until one of my journeys to the ashram coincided with one Cuth's later visits there in 1981 that I had the pleasure of meeting him. A scene vivid in my memory from that time is the broad back of the big Swede kneeling in front of Swami's open doorway to the verandah of the Mandir. I could see only Swami's face above the grey head of the kneeling figure. Mother Sai was smiling with gentle sweetness while giving pats on the shoulder to the kneeling figure. It was somehow an unforgettable picture.

Soon after that the Swede disappeared from the ashram, a fact I regretted because I had not had much chance to talk to him personally. But those who had known him during his earlier visits spoke to me about him. I gained the impression that he was generally regarded as a devotee of considerable status. Much of his fame seems centred around his power as a meditator. Swami, they said, had asked him to give a lecture on this subject to some of the college students. Such talk stirred my curiosity about the big gentle Swede. And so it was with some eagerness that I approached his printed story.

In one chapter he writes about his lessons from Swami in the art of meditation and describes how through following diligently the Sai teachings on this subject, he was able to reach wonderful levels of cosmic consciousness and experience cosmic visions. There are many highlights in the book which is a personal document full of significant experiences and much deep spiritual understanding.

It is written with sincerity and humility. On the whole his story reveals the author to me as one of those whom Emerson calls, "meek lovers of the good". In the constantly growing body of Sai literature, emanating from many different countries, this book by the admirable Swede is due to take an important place. With confidence I can recommend it, not only to Sai devotees, but also to the general public. Among the latter today there is an increasing number searching out with hungry hearts for the doorway that will take them away from the screaming madness of the world into the walled garden of peace, holy understanding and spiritual sustenance. I feel that this book will prove to be the right doorway for many searchers and thus become a powerful instrument in the work of the great Avatar, which I'm sure my good Sai Swedish friend meant it to be.

Howard Murphet

Blue Mountains NSW Australia

March 1992.

CONTENTS

Part I

We are Born with Three Identities

One identity is that of the body. It comes into existence through fertilization and seems to remain "ours" throughout the life-span. Finally the body decays and is annihilated after the heart ceases to beat. We are bound to the body and its functions and cannot escape from them. Thus we seem powerless but to accept diseases and injuries. We are unable to escape the infirmities of old age, our skin loses its elasticity, our bones become brittle, our hair loses its lustre, our limbs become heavier. Even the wisest philosopher cannot prevent by argument his body from inexorably growing older. And similarly the richest person cannot buy freedom from the final annihilation of the body.

The creating and all life maintaining energy is always the same - uninfluenced, undiminished, eternal. This all-comprising power is what we worship and in everyday speech term God. Our life and its span is highly dependent on the level of development of our consciousness. Through ignorance and an unreasonable way of living we generate bodily and mental imbalances. This is often the basic reason for the deterioration of the body through disease and accidents which prematurely shorten the span of our life.

The human body is a wonder of biological architecture, perfect in its ingenious construction right to its minutest details. A temple may be erected by a Master Designer. But if the intention is to build in its automatic self destruction over a period of time, then not even the aid of mechanical props to prevent the decay can stop the pillars from collapsing little by little and turning into dust. So it is with the body, which as a temple is something tremendous, something powerful, something wonderful, but only so long as it exists.

Consequently the body identity cannot be changed. From the cradle to the grave we own the same skin which envelops the same bowels, the same vein system, the same bones. A paradox exists here - everything is changed with the passage of time, but remains yet the same. When the body has ceased to exist, so also this identity no longer exists. What is left are only the memories of those who lived close to us, but when they have also physically departed from this world, what is there that can remind others of our body as it was? Nothing! There may be photographs, paintings, even a film clip, but these are only pale copies from only brief episodes of our life. Five minutes after a photo had been taken you were no longer the same person, because your body grew older during those five minutes.

Realization about the impermanence of our body, to which we seem to have such a strong in-born attachment, comes often very late in life. For the child a summer holiday is endless, a paradise that has no end. The young have their fermentation period when everything can happen, everything must be done, one can do everything and has the strength to do everything. The present seems to exist without end, whilst the future is ever distant. One refuses to believe that one will grow old. One imagines that the young, flexible body one has will always remain so. Intuitively most young people believe that they are exceptions, able to defy becoming old.

In middle age one becomes more and more aware how time flies and how short the allotted span of earthly life is in reality. For elderly people each and every day is a gift. The foolish grieve over their vanished youth, and those still more foolish curse their bodily fate. But those who, with equanimity, accept the changes have the best possibility of finding the fleeting, but none-the-less apparent, happiness that identification with the body can give.

The second identity is the one that lies in the genes. The set of qualities, talents, gifts and bodily appearance are uniquely yours and nobody else's. How you will appear as a grown-up is programmed in the foetus. You can do little about it. If your genes have determined that you shall become a person short in stature, you will be short. By your own efforts you can never add a single inch to your height. If it is determined that you shall have blue eyes, they will never become brown. If there exists an artistic talent in the genes, you can devote your life to art. If however you lack that talent it may be possible, through training, to achieve an ability to manage the most simple artistic forms, but it may be a waste of time and likely you will never become more than a feeble amateur.

Likewise, whether you will turn out to be an evil or a good person is also partly determined from the beginning. But when it comes to these kind of qualities, which relate to the inner nature rather than any physical attributes, you do have possibilities to influence this aspect of identity. In your spectrum of qualities there exists the whole scale from goodness to evil, and it is your own choice which qualities you wish to emphasize. But your choice is not entirely free. If you are born in an environment that is evil, and the people around you are evil, or if you are exposed to an environment of constant evil devoid of love, the chances are that you will possibly also become an evil person. But in any case, you have the possibility to change your own situation. If in the midst of this evil, you meet a good person in whose presence you can be so strongly influenced that from that moment on the evil vanishes, the goodness latent in you will come to dominate. The essence of our real nature is goodness, and love is our true being. The worst criminal, who has been regarded as a wild monster, unaffected by anything good previously, can become exposed to the love of a good fellow-being and can be transformed into an exemplary member of society. Similarly he can meet love in the form of a divine vision, and from that moment on start a new way of living.

The contrary can also happen. A person with the best of conditions for developing into a good person can be transformed into something that can be regarded as a devil. Vices have a tempting effect on many and can be experienced as difficult to resist. One of the best writers on this subject is Robert Louis Stevenson in his book "Dr. Jekyll and Mr. Hyde." It tells about a very good man, Karen Jekyll, who wants to search into the nature of evil and invents a drug that cultivates the evil qualities in the person who takes it. The intention was to use this drug on criminals thereby obtaining the opposite effect. The proposed subject of his experiment dies in prison before the drug is ready for a test, and Dr. Jekyll cannot resist the temptation to test it on himself. Thereby the saintly London Doctor becomes transformed into a malignant being never seen before even in the lower world of the metropolis. What is still worse, he derives pleasure from his evil deeds. Of course, the book can be read as an exciting novel. But Stevenson is really describing the tendencies in the nature of a human being where there is a constant fight between good and evil. If one gives way to the evil, yields to its enticing temptations, good and elevating qualities disappear and one is headed for one's own moral ruin. Every day we have to make hundreds, maybe thousands, of choices, and every choice is of importance for our personal development. We choose whom we shall meet, what we shall eat, what we shall read, what we shall talk about, what we are aiming at, what dreams we shall allow ourselves, what we must avoid and what we shall search for.

Our gene identity dies with the body identity. As an individual we do not exist anymore. The talents, the gifts, the qualities that were given to you in the primary hour of this incarnation have served their purpose during the time lived on Earth and they are destroyed with your body.

This does not mean after death it doesn't matter how you made use of your second identity. If you chose goodness, you have also influenced others to become good, as goodness is a quality aimed for by most people. If through your example you have shown that it is possible to live as a good person, others may follow your example and try to live in a similar way.

Even if your body identity is entirely unique, there are also some common features for all of us. For instance, we are born with one head, two arms, two legs, and so on. Likewise, in the genes unique to each individual there are common traits which are found in all other genes. No-one becomes three metres in height, or has violet eyes. The qualities we inherit are known and recognised.

Common to us all is also the yearning for something beyond the two identities that we are born with. From the beginning all are seekers. We possess an intuitive understanding that there must be something more to life than only being born, indulging the senses and then dying. In all cultures in all times there has been that search. Different answers have been found corresponding to the needs of different individuals. But the answer always revealed the awareness of a higher being, who is omnipotent, the creator of all, and to whom reverence is paid.

In many parts of the world secularisation has resulted in the erroneous belief that there exists nothing more than pure materialism. This has made people spiritually poor and unhappy. Yet there is still that seeking as a mighty force in people, even in countries where governments discourage spiritual/religious activities. For instance, when the Pope has visited East European countries ruled by dictatorships he has been welcomed by hundreds of thousands of people shouting with joy. Those in power have wisely chosen not to intervene, for that would have possibly resulted in uprisings and unwanted chaos.

In the north-western countries of Europe secularisation has also resulted in the disappearance of religious passion where strong feelings can transform a person. In such a state of upliftment a person can be carried into other spheres and brings about wondrous happenings. Unfortunately, here passion is exchanged for lukewarm small coins. The voice of conscience is not heard. In the mad pursuit of material gain one does not care about anybody or anything else, except what benefit one can derive for oneself. One floats with the current, does not discriminate and take a moral stand and is careful not to show religious passion of any kind. Common sense is the leading star now used in all spheres. Through discussion one reaches a solution to everything, valid in business, as in love and religious practice. But common sense has nothing to do with emotional life. When one feels the strong urge of passionate, or divine love, energy is released which creates the conditions for deeper insight into spiritual reality. It is this passion that makes a person forget everything else except merging in the object of one's feeling. One wants to be one with another, indivisibly grown together, one wants unification, and that becomes the most important thing in life. In religious passion this happens with the divinity one worships. A holy person, an incarnated divine being, can awaken such a storm of emotion, such a passion, that one becomes entirely dominated thereby. It is this passion that frees the higher emotions and shows the prodigious way to a new life.

This common, intuitive seeking for something beyond what can be seen, heard or understood with the five senses leads us to our third identity, the only one that is indestructible and eternal, the spirit, in esoteric terms called also the Atma, the soul. It can be called so since these conceptions are well founded. Our individual soul, our consciousness, follows us from bodily envelope to bodily envelope and, depending on how we lead our life, what choices we make, it develops in different ways. The soul is part of the cosmic energy and is included in the eternal universe. Each soul is a fraction of God, and consequently each human being is also divine.

To learn to know one's third identity much effort is required. If one has insight, is aware of one's atma, one's soul, the two first identities become less significant, of minor importance when compared with the third one. This is the reason we are given many periods of life in the timeless cycle of birth and death, for the development of the individual consciousness, our real I, our soul. Sai Baba explains our three identities by saying that one is what we think we are, another is the one others think we are, and the third is the One we really are.

This book will deal principally with this concept, and I shall later go more thoroughly into it. At the age of 50 I was mature enough to meet my spiritual teacher Bhagavan Sri Sathya Sai Baba in India. It would be helpful if I first tell about my life before I met Him, a life that consisted of seeking, though I did not exactly know what I was seeking for. This gradually allowed me to mature to the point where Sai Baba called me to come to Him to enable Him to guide my spiritual development.

My life in my first and second identity is, of course, of minor interest, except as a description of how man finds his way. It is of no interest for me either. I feel as if my first birth was unimportant, whereas my second birth after meeting Sai Baba is all important. And yet I consider that the features in the first phase of my life, which I considered unique, can be regarded as commonly valid to others also. Some may recognise themselves, and those who have felt themselves not yet ready to devote their time and energy to their spiritual development may be helped to take the first steps in this direction. This is my hope and the reason for telling a little about what I only find boring - my life before I met Sai Baba.

I was born in Southern Sweden. As a young child I often felt like an outsider, a different kind of child. It was in those days, as now, a time permeated with materialism. It was generally held that the first duty of a person was to see to it that he or she procured economic security and preferably also an influential position in society. All this was, however, entirely alien to my nature. I dreamt of being a painter, a student of philosophy, a writer and poet, something, of course, most people shook their heads at.

The one in the family I had a closer inner contact with was my grandmother. Next to illiterate she was an 'old' wise soul. At that time I did not realize it, but today I understand that she was my first spiritual teacher and prepared me for what later would come to characterize my life.

Already very early I felt a strong yearning for God, and when I read a book about Paramahamsa Yogananda, "Autobiography of a Yogi," a deep impression was made on me. Yogananda was an Indian spiritual Master who lived and worked in the Western World for more than 30 years, mainly in the United States, where he established The Self Realization Fellowship. His books have attracted great attention and have been translated into many languages.

This was my first conscious contact with Indian spiritual thinking, and I prayed to God that one day He would let me come to India and meet an enlightened Master, somebody who could give me spiritual inspiration and lead me to find the Truth.

Otherwise most of my childhood and youth has been repressed from my awareness. I preferred being alone amidst nature, God's law-bound creation, and I fantasized about travelling to other countries and learning about other peoples and other cultures. And so it turned out to be. I have travelled several times around the world, have seen and heard and experienced other living conditions. I have travelled with an open mind and taken in the teachings which these international studies have presented. There were two countries which I especially had dreamt of seeing, India and Egypt, and both of them were just as fascinating as I had imagined.

When I was 19 years old I became severely ill and had to undergo a complicated back-operation. This forced me to stay for more than a year with little physical activity. This proved to be a useful time as far as my spiritual development was concerned. I realized that there was no use in moping around and feeling pity for myself. This was a test, a challenge which I could come through greatly strengthened if I took advantage of my opportunities.

To learn one has to make one's mistakes. I was far from ready and I would have to be knocked and soaked, kneaded and rolled, before I was mature for my second birth.

Amongst other qualities a great stubbornness and a strong willpower of rather unusual degree were part of my genes. Whatever I decided to do I then put in a great effort and was successful. It seemed that I was fortunate to recognize these qualities and made best use of them. That is what one tries to do if one has this turn of mind. One and one always make two.

I had met a woman I wanted to share my life with. She displayed both inner (spiritual) and outer (worldly) qualities and came from a family in Finland with generations of spiritual seekers. We felt that we belonged together and that there was a deeper meaning to life after we had met.

I had started art studies in the Art College in Stockholm, and was determined to become an artist. All of a sudden I then happened to overhear a remark made to my wife from a close family member. Although it was not meant for my ears,I heard the following words, "Poor one, he will never be able to support you." My stubbornness was at once aroused, that stubbornness that originates from boyish immaturity. "I shall indeed show them. . ." I would demonstrate to the family, even though I did not share the same materialistic traits that they had, or expected, that they were wrong about me. I would indeed be able to support my wife!

So, instead of painting and writing I became a businessman and used all my will-power and energy for gathering worldly riches. I learnt the written and the unwritten rules that are valid in business, and soon put them into practise. I worked hard and was successful in my endeavours.

The principles of business were firmly in my control. Even though I changed my line of business several times, each time, within a relatively short period I became successful. It seemed easy. I made bargains, procured favourable contacts, played the game, made my moves, smiled where I had to smile, agreed where it was necessary, was hard where it was necessary for the bargain, was soft where it was profitable. I found my way to the right persons and formulated for myself beneficial agreements. In the bank the money grew and my fame as a successful businessman increased, for which I was shown great respect. But it was for me like living under a glass cover. The business world was not the real one for me, it was like a strange dream.

On arriving home after each day's work I meditated a while and the day's worries ran off me like dirty water. In my meditation I experienced glimpses of the cosmic reality. I understood that business was not my path. I also intuitively understood that I had to get all these experiences and learnings which were necessary for my development. My cup, which had been filled with a cloudy bitter drink, had to be emptied to the last drop before it could be filled with pure and clear water. And always I felt that a change was slowly going on within me. I was more and more dissatisfied with my daily activities that did not give me anything other than more money.

I understood that one who only aims at becoming rich is obstructing his or her spiritual development. A person with an undeveloped soul is a stunted being. The melody of gold is deceiving to listen to, and anyone who yields to it runs the risk of being drowned in the same way as the rats in the story of the Pied Piper of Hamelin. One has one's friends, but most of them are only friends in appearance. One thinks one is talking about essential subjects, but they are worth less than the grains of sand on a deserted beach. One considers that the work at hand is important, but in a wider perspective than the gilded, the stunted, it doesn't even exist.

Much evil comes from greed. It distorts worthwhile feelings, blunts compassion, kills sympathy and love; it poisons understanding of the plight of others. For those who worship gold as their god, consciousness is lost of the real self within. One who seeks for wealth is often blinded by greed. Around me I saw many who believed success was a matter of luck. Some of them thought that success in business was something they had deserved, was their fate, and thus looked down upon those who did not have similar success. The proverb says, "Business is business," and that can excuse everything else. The role models to be followed, the gods so to speak, in this game of business mostly have no regard for true spirituality. They are honoured even though they may be the hardest by nature, the coldest in emotion, the most intelligent in a secular way, or the most wealthy.

No, I'm not proud of this phase of my life, but it was necessary for me to go through. It was my childhood disease that I had to suffer to evolve to a more spiritually sound person.

During all this time I felt there was something else that was meant for me and that the activities I was engaged in were only stations on the journey. The inner feeling, the intuition I call God's voice, talked to me and I listened. And yet my inner hearing was not sufficiently developed to enable me to fully understand and interpret the message.

During my first journey to the Far East we made a short stop-over in Bombay to refuel and thereafter we flew over the holy land of India en-route to Thailand. It was early morning, the sun broke through the belt of mist and I was able to look down and catch a first glimpse of the goal of my yearning. The soul of India and my soul met. Though I was above the land at a height of thousands of metres, my heart was filled with love and warmth.

Since then I have visited India six times and stayed there for long periods of time, and each time my first impression of personal connection was strengthened. I do not think it is possible to feel such a love and kinship, such a deep happiness of reunion, such a reverence and respect for a country, its people and culture, without there being a deeper reality and meaning to it. When I came to India it was like returning home after a long journey.

For most Westerners India can be confusing with its strange way of living and entirely different culture. Thus many Westerners are never able to accustom themselves to India. For them the West with its values, which equates the striving for material possessions with happiness, has the only correct perspective. But for me everything was familiar, what I saw in India I had seen before, what I heard was well known to me. What others perceived as noise and confusion was a collection of sounds that built up a normal picture of the pattern of city life. The strange scents that were alien to the noses of other Westerners were familiar to me.

The only explanation that made sense was that I had lived in India in a previous life. We human beings have had many previous lives here on Earth, in various places. We have to develop on the plane we are born on to learn the lessons of life. Through meditation we can reach the deep stillness that is necessary for us to learn to know our true self, the real I, which is God, and thereby find the bonds to earlier incarnations. My daily meditation practices have led me to the spiritual development that made it possible for me to be able to perceive in India the vibrations from the person I once had been there.

In the autumn of 1979 my wife Sisko and I planned a vacation trip to the United States. I was rather exhausted and felt that I needed a holiday which included being in the sun, bathing and rest. Therefore we chose California and Hawaii as our destination. Then God intervened in my life. Many people imagine that everything happens at random, but this is not so. There are no coincidences or chances. Everything is an ingeniously woven pattern and everything has a meaning that can be hidden from us. Since this meaning is, to the uninitiated, hidden, we therefore often seem to make wrong choices, we misinterpret what happens.

Some time earlier I obtained, through a good friend, a book entitled "Man of Miracles" written by Howard Murphet. It dealt with Sathya Sai Baba, and having read the first chapter I felt intuitively a strange and strong attraction towards this spiritually highly developed Master. I read the book in excitement, put it aside for a while and tried to digest that bewildering and overwhelming experience. Thereafter I re-read the book, but with greater reflection.

Suddenly it was clear that Sai Baba was the spiritual teacher, the guru, whom I so eagerly had asked God for. This moment was the great turning-point in my life. I would go to India and I would try to meet Sai Baba. My strong yearning for learning to know and experience the Truth, God, had led me to the Avatar Sri Sathya Sai Baba.

I read the book a third time, and I felt Sai Baba calling me on each page. It was a book written about Him, but He spoke directly to me through it. Yes, I would go to India to meet this spiritual Master! Nothing would stop me!

Bhagavan Sri Sathya Sai Baba

Who is this intriguing Sai Baba! This whole book will deal with my path to Sai Baba, my relationship with Sai Baba, and thus how He helped me to a new and spiritual life.

Bhagavan Sri Sathya Sai Baba was born on November 23rd, 1926, in the small village of Puttaparthi in Andhra Pradesh, a state in Southern India, about 160 kilometres north of Bangalore city. As a new born child He was named Sathyanarayana. He was born, a divine incarnation, to awaken our love for each other and for God.

Sathyanarayana attended the village school like the other children and it is recorded that He was an exemplary pupil. He demonstrated remarkable gifts for music and poetry as well as writing and performing drama. At the tender age of eight years He wrote songs for short plays with spiritual content. From the beginning it was clear to most people that He was not like the other children. He was a mature human being even as a child and could see through falsehood and hypocrisy.

Sathyanarayana was loved by all because He radiated a goodness that could be sensed by the recipient with great intensity. Also He possessed powers which the ignorant call supernatural, but which for a divine being are quite natural. He had the gift to materialize objects from nowhere and amused his friends by creating items such as fruits, sweets or school writing materials.

Persons trained in a traditional scientific way, without knowledge of spiritual life, would declare this to be impossible. How is it possible to create something out of nothing? Consequently, Sai Baba must be a trickster, merely a show magician, an illusionist who has learnt many tricks to deceive the sight. It is not part of the education of a Westerner to believe in something other than what he can immediately see and touch.

However there are several pictures of reality, and if one accepts only one of them, one is stunting oneself and limiting one's vision including one's possibilities to get insight into other levels of consciousness. In India, on the other hand, a land that is permeated with religious feeling, materialization is not even questioned as it is accepted quite naturally. The doubts of Westerners are not understood and are regarded as insensitive and incongruous.

An incarnated divinity, an Avatar like Sai Baba, is born with the knowledge of who He is, what His mission is and what gifts He possesses. He is God in a human body, but nevertheless a complete expression of God. Since all are created in accordance with God's plan and in the imaes of God, we are also fragments of divinity. Sai Baba often says that we and He are all God, whereas He is aware that He is God we are not. An Avatar possesses knowledge about the inexplicable. Westerners often regard the supernatural as incredible. In India the inexplicable need not be explained, one does not need to see or touch everything in order to have an intuitive understanding about it.

The performance of miracles by an Avatar is only in conformity with His task and has as its aim the strengthening of bonds between Him and those who believe in Him. Materialization of objects is a natural means for spiritual communication. But , says the Westerner, it is contrary to all physical laws to take a concrete object out of thin air. This cannot be done. But what is "a concrete object?" What is "thin air?" What is "something?" What is "nothing?" Even in Western science the theory of indestructibility of energy is accepted as axiomatic. Nothing can be annihilated, matter is only transformed into another form. A piece of ferrous stone can be heated, mixed with carbon and thereby transformed into partly steel and partly slag. The one element only becomes two others by being influenced by a third, namely carbon, as well as a fourth, fire. All these constituents are energy in free or bound forms.

A piece of granite is not a dead object, but consists of molecules and atoms which give it such an appearance. When feeling cold one seeks warmth from fire. The wood is burnt in the process but does not disappear, it is transformed into heat, a form of energy which the cold person absorbs. Another example is when one opens his or her mouth to shout. For the sound to emerge one uses both muscle energy and lung energy which in turn are transformed into sound. But then sound is waves in the air. Even if it doesn't reach a human ear to be transformed to hearing energy it is still there and unites with other forms of energy, some of which may be inert.

Everything that has taken place in the world we know is stored somewhere. All groaning, all complaining, all laughter, all words, all the cries of younger children, all sighs from the aged, all the uproar from battles, even the silent prayers for peace - none of these have vanished, except for our hearing which is limited by time and space. It can be all around us, it can move out into the cosmos. What we did, what we said and what we thought has not lost its existence, but has only gone over into another form of energy.

An Avatar like Sai Baba has the power at will to transform free energy into bound energy. An invisible energy becomes in His hands a visible object. Energy is the primeval force which is the basis for all life. Without energy there would be no oxygen for us to inhale and transform into nitrogen through breathing, another form of energy. In India this has been understood for thousands of years. Western discoveries in this field in recent years, some of which are sensationalised, are looked upon with astonishment in India. The attitude in India is that at last the West has 'discovered' that which has been known to its Saints and Sages from time immemorial. Even for a mature Western spiritual seeker it can take time to come to terms with the Avatar Sai Baba's miracles which are deeply anchored to the Indian philosophy of religion.

And finally, in this context, let us put the question to the sceptic, a question that can be logically understood: "What would Sai Baba gain by bluffing?" Sai Baba has not built His work on miracles. It is built on love, love and love, on the conviction that life can be changed, that all people possess possibilities to transform themselves for the better. The miracles, the materializations, are of secondary importance to Sai Baba, and it is mainly the Westerners who wonder at them. His Indian devotees look upon them as natural phenomena.

But thousands of people see them happen every day. Over the years millions and millions of persons have witnessed these miracles. Materializations can be seen on thousands of photographs, they can be seen in numerous films and video productions. Pictures have been enlarged to the maximum and examined, films have been run at a slow pace. Non-believers, doubters, have taken up the task to unmask Sai Baba, with the aim to be the one who has discovered the "deceit." However, none has been successful. These persons have in fact achieved the opposite - they proved that no tricks exist, that the miracles are genuine.

With all the enormous attention which Sai Baba is subjected to, including work conducted through the various wings of His Organization, the result of Him being exposed using one trick would mean the end of all His activities. This could cause everything to collapse. His organization would not survive that day. But this does not happen. His devotees continue to receive pictures of Him, materialized out of the atmosphere, as well as lockets and vibhuti (holy ash). Sai Baba will never be "exposed," because there is nothing to expose. His life's work has not collapsed. On the contrary, it gains in strength from day by day, year after year, because the number of His devotees keeps growing all the time. His love attracts more and more people in a world thirsting for divine love.

A seeking but still distrustful Westerner needs to decide within himself or herself whether to go further. This aspirant should accept these miracles as trifles in a vaster plan and say, "With the spiritually barren and secular education I had at home and school, and the generally unspiritual environment I have grown up in, I cannot yet understand everything. I will put it aside until a later stage in order to try to penetrate what is of greater value for me, the development of my soul. Perhaps the other question will be answered little by little, or perhaps, in the overall scheme it may no longer be important."

Or, he or she has to say, "I cannot believe in what must be hocus pocus, as I cannot fathom how it is done. And since I cannot believe in this, I refuse to believe in the integrity of the person behind the acts. If there is trickery in one, there is bound to be also in the other. It is either true or false, there is nothing in-between." But taking such an attitude means that such aspirants have also come to a standstill in their spiritual journey. Only those who search for something have a chance to find something. Searching means to receive and accept new experiences, to learn from other's wisdom and knowledge and let these merge in one's own.

This book is written for such seekers and discoverers, for all those who realize that even when one accepts what one does not fully comprehend, or finds strange regarding the vision of the path through life, still one has taken a step forward.

The young Sathya continued His schooling in Uravakonda, and His teachers saw in Him their equal in knowledge and their superior in wisdom. As an Avatar He could see into the past and into the future, and for His schoolmates He stood out as their guru - spiritual teacher - even at that time.

At the time of birth an Avatar is already aware of His earthly task, and at given points of time takes up a new phase of His mission. He knows what has to be done and when He has to start His work. When Sathya was fourteen years old the time was ripe for Him to set about the task that He had undertaken. He threw away His school books. He explained to His nearest family members, "I'm no longer your Sathya. I am Sai Baba. I'm going now. I do not belong to you any longer. My devotees are waiting for Me. I have My work to do. I cannot stay any longer." Nobody opposed Him. Nobody asked Him to continue His education. They knew that this had to happen. Sai Baba belonged to all people, and what He had set out to do could not be learnt in any books.

As soon as that declaration was made there were already followers, for when Sai Baba spoke people listened, and when they had listened, they felt impelled to follow Him. He had a radiation of divine goodness that was impossible to resist. Out of His own free will He had incarnated to teach us to live together in love, truth, righteousness and peace.

This famous declaration occurred in 1940, and from that time on the small unknown village of Puttaparthi and Sai Baba's Ashram, named Prasanthi Nilayam (Abode Of Highest Peace), have become well known all over the world. The Ashram has expanded considerably and includes an extremely beautiful temple, referred to as the Mandir, the Poornachandra Auditorium, which can hold over twenty thousand people, a pre-school, primary school, high school and University complex, a modern planetarium. There is even a well-equipped hospital, as well as a dairy farm, which serves as a model farm in the district, and a number of residential and associated facilities for the benefit of visitors and residents alike. To this day the Ashram and Educational Complexes are continually expanding to meet the needs of the growing numbers coming to be with Sai Baba.

Besides this Sai Baba has established several ashrams, hospitals, schools and universities for both sexes in various parts of India. The Sai Organization has today many millions of active members in about a hundred countries all over the world.

And it was this Avatar whom I felt I had to meet. It was He who held my future life in His hands. I had to tell my wife Sisko about this and thought that she might have some objections. On one hand she had not yet read about Sai Baba and on the other, I knew what hard experiences our two earlier visits to India had been for her.

India is a country with enormous contrasts. There is the peace, the wisdom - but also the pain, distress, poverty, starvation and misery. Everything makes such a strong impression that one cannot escape it. As one is amidst the Indian maelstrom one has to see and hear all the various expressions of suffering. Sisko is a person of soft heart, warmth and compassion, and she felt a hopelessness, a powerlessness, when facing all this distress and disease. She became almost paralysed and could not enjoy all the evidences of India's enormous cultural history, which this huge country has to offer. Everywhere she found marks of suffering and these followed her in her dreams.

Not until we left the country did she feel she could breathe freely again and she said to me, "No more visits to India! I cannot manage it!" And yet - we had both felt great reverence for the true and profound spirituality which in its pristine glory lay beyond suffering and poverty in this holy country.

I told Sisko about Sai Baba and my wish to return to India instead of going to the United States. I was happy, but not surprised, upon hearing her spontaneous answer, "If you want to see Sai Baba, then let us do it!" She then read the book about Sai Baba and we discussed the contents with growing conviction that it was God who called us again to India. My yearning was so strong that my being ached to know the Truth. I had been prepared for this journey, but at this time was not aware of it. I had not been able to interpret the signs.

Before we left Sweden I often meditated and Sai Baba's picture became clearer and clearer in my heart of hearts. On one such occasion I smelt a strange, strong scent in the room. After meditation I got up to find the reason for this scent, but it had disappeared and I could find no explanation. Later on in India I learnt to recognise the scent of incense sticks and remembered the experience I had in Sweden. In this way Sai Baba bade me welcome. But, as already said, I did not know that.

It is a long way to India and there was much to be arranged before we could depart. Those days preparing for the trip were filled with enthusiasm and excitement. We talked about Sai Baba and were so filled with Him though we had not yet seen Him in flesh and blood that these weeks felt unreal, like a fragmentary dream. We booked air tickets, arranged for visas and packed, but it was our voices and hands that arranged all that, our souls were already on the other side of the globe.

None the less, our bodies had to move in the usual way, and we had been used to all the comforts that our modern society offered. Now much was otherwise. The journey turned out to be very tiresome, and we had little option but to rest in the most primitive hotels or lodgings. In Madras we even had to spend a night without a bed. Instead we had to sit on a hard chair till morning dawned.

These were hardships, but when faced and overcome, were forgotten. Perhaps Sai Baba wanted to test the strength of our desire to come to Him. But not even earthquakes, floods or rain of fire and sulphur could have stopped our journey.

At last we arrived in Bangalore and were able to have a few days' rest before taking a taxi to our destination, Sai Baba's Ashram in Puttaparthi. The taxi ride took about three hours under the hot dry sun of India. But for every mile travelled in the car we were closer to Him.

When we arrived the sun had already begun to set and it was a little easier for us Northerners to breathe, as we were not used to the Indian climate. Before being able to think of anything else we had to slake our thirst, but we had to be very careful with what we drank, as the strange bacteria flora could be too much for our sensitive stomachs. In more than one way we were like children, when first arriving at Prasanthi Nilayam.

And then we entered the temple compound. There was a hammering in my brain, "We are in Sai Baba's Ashram!" In spite of the fruit drink it was difficult to swallow. As is customary in this part of the world and in this culture the men and women were separated from each other, each with their own segregated area, and Sisko went over to where the ladies were.

There was a large number of men seated on the ground in several lines, and they sat in the Eastern way with crossed legs. Because of my back problem, I was not able to sit like that. Therefore I placed myself at some distance, from where I had a good view over the whole beautiful temple compound. Some men were talking quietly with each other, when suddenly there was an electrifying atmosphere. Immediately all became silent and turned their heads towards the Mandir.

And there stood Sai Baba! He! The Swami! My guru! He was dressed in His red robe, but for a while I could not recognize the colour. My heart pounded in my breast as if trying to break the ribs, the heat still in the air was like a lead weight on my shoulders and I felt dizziness. How I had longed to see Him! Now I could not be more than a few metres away from where He stood!

"I'm lucky not to be sitting in the first line," rushed through my giddy brain. "At least where I was He was unlikely to come. But if. . . . . if He broke the line and came up to me? No, I couldn't handle that! I was not ready for that. I would not be able to control myself. I would start crying, because I did not know of any other means of giving vent to the feelings pulsating through my entire being. No, Sai Baba, not today! Not now! It is too early! Let me stay in the background and only take in Your appearance!"

My wish was fulfilled, and my first impression of Sai Baba's nearness was overwhelming. He walked along the long lines of men and women and gave His darshan - blessing - to all the devoted followers who were sitting in worship and expectation. Many of them had letters in their hands which they held out towards Him, hoping that He would receive them. In most of the letters there was the same wish, a prayer asking for a personal conversation with Sai Baba. Many have had to wait for weeks or for months. Many have had to repeat their prayer several times, before they were granted a divine interview, a conversation that is regarded as a great grace.

It is only Sai Baba Himself who decides with whom He wants to talk. There are those who sometimes try to buy priority, but this does not work. It is vain effort. Others try to obtain His compassion through pretence of acute sickness, or lack of time. But Sai Baba cannot be forced into anything. He is not to be bought. He cannot be blackmailed. His divine vision is able to penetrate who for various reasons are in greatest need of a personal talk, and they always come first.

Now I could see Him exchange words with some people, and His gentle smile implied so much goodness that I felt a lump in my throat. For some He materialized vibhuti by raising His right hand and making a few circles in the air. One could not miss seeing the enormous happiness and gratitude that the people in the temple compound felt in His presence. Now I was within the sphere of this all-embracing warm spirit of community! After Sai Baba had completed His darshan, His round of blessings, He returned to the temple as the evening bhajans commenced. Bhajans are group devotional songs sung in worship to God.

When the last tone had died away it was time for Sisko and me to take a well-needed rest. The day had indeed been physically strenuous and psychically demanding. We had rented a small room in the village without a window and without adequate ventilation. We lay on our thin mattresses on the stone floor, which soon became a torment to our unaccustomed bodies. Then there also were the heat and mosquitoes which didn't leave us alone. And also the thirst, as we had neglected to take with us into the room enough water for the night. The result was too little sleep and too little rest.

In spite of this we were filled with Sai Baba. We had seen Him and we knew that He was not far away from where we were lying on the stone floor. Maybe He smiled at our troubles with our heavy Northern bodies, used to eider-down and air conditioning!

When morning dawned even these hardships were forgotten. We had a shower, some good tea and looked at each other. Sisko could read my thoughts, and impulsively she took my hand. "I think He will talk to you today!" We went together to the temple compound to be seated for the morning darshan. Once more Sisko squeezed my hand, before she went over to the ladies' side. I had borrowed a chair, and when I arrived the volunteers made room for me in the first line.

At half past nine it suddenly again became quiet. The only thing to be heard was the light wind playing with the leaves in the tree tops. Sai Baba came out of the temple and went towards a volunteer who stood at the temple porch, opposite the place where I was sitting, and exchanged some words with him. At the same time He looked at me and I could see that His intention was to come towards me. Feelings overwhelmed me in the same way as the evening before, as I had been afraid they would do. The powerful light and the tremendous vibrations that emanated from Sai Baba influenced me to such a degree that I understood that I would behave in an unworthy manner. I whispered in silence, "Wait! Wait, Sai Baba!" - obviously He understood and stayed a few more moments with the volunteer.

"Control yourself!" I told myself. "You are at the goal of your dreams. Your intensive yearning has come true. Sai Baba wants you to behave suitably. Justify His confidence in you!" Slowly I then felt that I again was capable of behaving in a proper way in His presence, and I was again able to breathe almost normally.

Sai Baba looked at me again and then He came straight towards me. For each step He took my heart throbbed an extra beat. And now .... now He stood before me - He, Sai Baba!

I Meet the Avatar Sri Sathya Sai Baba

Our eyes met. He asked from where I came and then asked me to go in for an interview.

The interview room was full to its capacity with expectant devotees. Sai Baba gave me a sign to follow Him into an adjacent more private room.

I felt giddy in His presence from the radiation of His love and light, and this made it difficult for me to comprehend all that He said. When He asked me if I wanted to have a locket with pictures of Sai Baba on one side and Shirdi Baba, His previous incarnation, on the other side, I felt a lump in my throat, tears were not far away. I was struggling to control myself and with a very emotional tinge responded, "Yes, thank You. I'd be very happy." Sai Baba asked me to look carefully at His outstretched hand and made a few circular movements in the air. When He opened His hand there lay the locket He had described for me, fixed to a chain. He hung it around my neck and said, "I'm always with you and this locket will protect you." Overwhelmed, and in great gratitude I bent down and kissed His divine Lotus Feet. This gesture was a spontaneous expression of the love that filled my heart.

Sai Baba understood that I was not able just then to receive more of His powerful divine radiation and asked if I wished to leave the room and go out. "I think so," was my answer. He gave me so many vibhuti packages that my pockets were virtually overfull and He accompanied me to the outer door.

Bewildered, I stood in the sunlight out in the temple compound. Sai Baba had touched my heart and it was difficult for me to control the feeling of happiness that filled me.

Many of the devotees gathered around me and asked how it came about that I had left the interview room, as all the others were still inside. Just at this moment I was unable to put into words what I felt and left their question unanswered. I had only one wish, to be left in peace, alone with my thoughts of Sai Baba!

I spent the day resting and pondered deeply over the divine blessing I had received in the morning. I pulled myself together and decided to write a letter to Sai Baba, a letter filled with gratitude that He had called me to come to Him. I wrote that I had come to Him only out of love for God, of a yearning to know the Truth, and with a hope that He in His grace and love would guide my spiritual development. I also wrote that when I stood before Him in the interview room the same morning enclosed in His divine love and light, I had felt that God was standing embodied before me. I was deeply moved, humbled and grateful that He had heard my prayers. During evening darshan Sai Baba came up to me and asked if I was happy. I gave Him my letter saying, "Yes, Sai Baba, I'm very happy."

On the last day of our one week long stay in Prasanthi Nilayam Sai Baba called us in the morning for what we thought would be a farewell interview. He asked me to sit down on a stool at His side and said that daily He receives many, many letters. Then He added, with a loving look at me, that my letter had made Him very happy.

Sai Baba knew that we were to leave early in the evening and asked us to once more come in to Him, at four o'clock that afternoon, before the evening darshan was to begin. When we arrived, the stool at His side was again reserved for me and Sisko sat on the floor in front of Him. Sai Baba asked Sisko what she wanted, and she answered, "Love, to share with people around me." Sai Baba immediately responded by materializing a small silver box with gold hearts on the lid. It was filled with vibhuti and He said that she should take a little vibhuti in water every evening as the climate and the long journey had been tiresome for her. Sisko asked if she could give a little vibhuti to friends who give a little vibhuti to friends who were in difficulties, which Sai Baba said that she could certainly do. Deeply moved and grateful Sisko kissed Sai Baba's hands.

For me Sai Baba materialized a beautiful silver ring with a portrait of Shirdi Baba and then asked us to step into the adjacent room which is more private. There He confirmed what I intuitively had felt, by saying, "You have lived very close to me in an earlier life." I also received a sheet with sixty adhesive small pictures of Sai Baba, and then He put His hand on my head saying, "I take away the darkness from your eyes." Love filled my heart and tears of happiness rolled down my cheeks. My entire inner being was filled with light, I was light. A sensation of love I shall never forget! Sai Baba said furthermore, "You shall soon come back and live here, near me." Overwhelmed by His love and grace I bent down to His Lotus Feet in deep humility and gratitude. With the words, "We shall meet again soon," Sai Baba accompanied us out of the interview room.

In the temple grounds Professor Bhagavantam came towards us to bid us farewell. "We shall soon see you again. I know that Sai Baba is waiting for you to return soon. I know that you have His grace and will experience a happy time here with Sai Baba. If there is anything I can help you with, do not hesitate to write to me. It is only a pleasure for me if I can do something for you." I was very happy and grateful for his kind offer. Professor Bhagavantam was a highly intelligent, humble and generous person, who later became my confidant and close friend. Later on he came to mean much to me. We took farewell for this time.

Our first visit to Sai Baba had come to an end. A taxi took us to Bangalore. We were both deeply sunk in our thoughts, grateful and happy at how much Sai Baba had let us experience His divine love. We both felt that we would soon return to Him in Puttaparthi.

Home in Sweden After the First Visit to Sai Baba

It was a welcome relief to come home to the cool climate in Sweden. We were in desperate need of rest from the psychic and physical strain the visit to India had imposed. Several weeks passed before we regained our normal strength and could begin to digest and work at all the spiritual experiences the stay with Sai Baba had given us.

It was difficult for relatives and friends to grasp and understand when we told them about what we had experienced. Some of our friends thought that we had been hypnotized into seeing what we saw, that Sai Baba was a skilful illusionist who had hidden in his robe the various objects He said He had materialized. But, we had often seen how He deliberately drew His sleeves up over the elbows to show that He did not hide anything.

There are numerous examples of sceptics and well-known magicians who have come to Sai Baba expressly to expose Him, but none of them has been successful nor been able to give any reasonable explanations for His materializations.

It has not been possible to prove that Sai Baba's materializations are tricks or magic. But what did all our explanations help! If one does not want to believe, one cannot believe.

When we told them how Sai Baba created lockets, rings and the like out of thin air before our eyes, we were met with shaking heads - such a thing just simply couldn't happen. The only answer we could give was that given by Sai Baba Himself, "Come, see Me, examine Me and become yourself convinced. I do not need to use tricks and magic. What I think of, that I create. What I will shall happen, that happens."

That Sai Baba is also able to transfer objects from far-away places He Himself has asserted and carried out. He has displayed things which He has transferred and explained where they came from. Often the object has been jewellery and statues of deities which are in various temples in India. Through temporarily transferring Sai Baba has "borrowed" these holy objects to reveal the special history and importance related to them. On many occasions He also said that through His handling of the objects they have had their spiritual potency regenerated. Afterwards He has let these objects return to their rightful place.

On another occasion a devotee who was visiting Sai Baba had complained that he had forgotten his glasses at home and now experienced difficulties in managing without them. "Don't worry, I shall fetch them for you," Sai Baba offered, and to the devotee's great surprise handed over his familiar glasses with the comment, "Well, you had forgotten them on the kitchen table," or something similar.

I shall not elaborate any further, but instead shall let Sai Baba Himself tell about His miracles in a later chapter.

Our days were filled with various activities, and we were fully occupied with preparations for our next journey to India, which we planned to take place within a couple of months. This time we planned to stay at least two months with Sai Baba. There were many arrangements to be made and questions of various kinds to ponder over. We tried also to make time to read and learn as much as possible about Indian culture, customs and habits, which now were of quite special interest to us. The difference between the cultural world we came from and that of India is extremely great.

Religion is deeply anchored in the Indian culture, contrary to the much more passive religiosity of Westerners. Our churches are often nearly empty, and religion plays a subordinate role. In our schools the teaching of religion has in some places entirely disappeared. In our industrially highly developed society material values are more appreciated than spiritual ones. We think our time is too precious to be offered to religion which, expressed in a modern way, is only looked upon as "opium for the people."

In a place of work some men made fun of a colleague who used to sit about ten minutes in prayer and meditation on God every morning and evening. Their argument was that one could not know if God really existed. "No," the man said, "maybe one cannot know that. But, if there is no God I have wasted twenty minutes of every day, whereas, if there is a God, you have wasted your whole life."

This materialistic attitude has strongly influenced the youth in our society. Morality and ethics are conceptions that do not play the same role they once did, and it is not difficult to see the negative effects of such an outlook on life. A small light to lead to change, however, can be seen today in various parts of the world. People are beginning to awake out of their Sleeping Beauty dream. The material prosperity which until now has played such a decisive and dominant role is beginning to be re-evaluated on account of the negative consequences the high-technological industrialization has brought about. The question is being asked, "What kind of world shall we leave behind for our children?"

In our lust for consumption we have not understood and considered that the unique life spring of nature may already have been irreparably damaged. "Has it been worth the price?" The answer must, of course, without the least hesitation be "No!" The cost has been far too great.

Let us hope that it is not too late to change this development before the damage to nature and the environment becomes so widespread and fatal that catastrophes of global dimension cannot any longer be avoided.

Towards A Clearer Consciousness

During our stay in India with Sai Baba, Sisko and I experienced how strongly we were bound to the habit of having all comforts within reach. We had to contend with circumstances, for example, where temperatures reached between 40-50°C, which were quite alien and thus very trying. The simple life of an ashram can easily create problems for a spoiled Westerner. But it was instructive to accept and live under these conditions. One learns humility and gratitude.

Sai Baba had opened our eyes and we became aware of many things which previously we had accepted as obvious, but now found not to be always so. Millions of people in India do not even have access to fresh water. They live under the scorching sun without that which is most necessary. Such experiences give us something to think about, how spoiled and ungrateful we often are. We learnt also how happy people can be to be able to appease their hunger at least once a day. These reminders, these experiences helped us to widen our understanding of the distress and needs of others, to not only think of ourselves, and taught us to share with our brothers and sisters, who were worse off, and feel humility face to face with all divine creation.

Yes, indeed, it was a revolutionary, an instructive stay with Sai Baba, in so many ways. With these insights we arrived home and learned to lighten considerably the material luggage we earlier had thought was necessary and had carried with us through our lives. Sai Baba had given us so much, which we now had to work on and assimilate. He had fiiled us in so many ways, our hearts were filled with His love, our thoughts with humble gratitude. Now it was time, with all our might, to start the arduous task to put these learnings into practice in our daily lives. We began to understand how self-centred we had been and that it was now high time to give of ourselves for helping and serving our brothers and sisters. We must become less selfish and understand that the suffering of another also is our suffering, another's happiness is our happiness.

There were many revolutionary and decisive decisions for me to make, which were not always easy. Sai Baba had told me to wind up my business engagements, to return soon. My place was with Him, I should live near Him. In any case, the year before I read and heard about Sai Baba I had started a certain degree of liquidation, and now I intensified this. I worked harder than I had done for a long time. But this did not stop me from getting up still earlier in the morning for devoting the earliest morning hours to stillness and meditation. This now had become more important, more meaningful since I had met and was guided by my divine guru Sai Baba.

Sai Baba is called Swami, Master. I thought of Him as God embodied in human form. It is we who give words their meaning, in accordance with what we feel in our heart, what we have in our thoughts.

Sisko made brave efforts to learn to cook vegetarian food. The result was indeed very tasteful and I was glad that I could commend her for her cooking. Sai Baba had given her a japamala, an Indian rosary, and she often retreated to her room. She lit a candle before Sai Baba's picture, sat awhile in stillness and made her japa, as Sai Baba with His own fingers had taught her. And I'm convinced that it was not only her fingers that were active! It was a great pleasure to see how seriously she was engaged in her work and how radiant with love when talking about Sai Baba. Well, I thought Sisko had become a real "Sai-devotee."

Our family and friends were not equally delighted with what I related after having met Sai Baba and the resultant changes in our daily lives. It didn't help when I tried to explain. They did not want to understand, they were not ready to be able to understand. They simply could not accept that I had a different way to go. Nowadays I choose carefully those I speak with about my beliefs.

In some of our old friends an interest in Sai Baba has been awakened, and I used to give them books to read in support of what we discussed. This has been fortunate, and we experience strongly Sai Baba's love and blessing.

On returning to Sweden after our first visit to Sai Baba, it was difficult for us to keep back the rich, revolutionary, emotional experiences that the personal contact with Him had meant to us. Our happiness and enthusiasm had no limits, but with the passing of time we learnt to control our feelings and to propound Sai Baba's message of love in a more balanced and discriminating way. We have found that the best way for awakening people's interest in Sai Baba's life and work is to try to practise in our own daily life His divine teachings. When people themselves begin to ask, the time is ripe to sow new thoughts in their minds and awaken love for all fellow-creatures in their hearts.

Sai Baba has helped us and guided us, so that we today have many old and new friends in the circle of Sai-love. This has caused many to change their earlier view of life and led to a deepened spiritual development. It is through all this I can now appreciate how Sai Baba guides us with love and grace.

The Second Visit to Sai Baba

My striving to know Sai Baba better brought about a great change in my daily life. This I had also said to Him during an interview He gave me in Puttaparthi. I remember that I said, "You have entirely changed my view of life. Meeting You means a great change in my future life." I also asked Him why He had not called me earlier. "You were not prepared and ready for coming to me earlier," was His reply. On second thoughts I began to understand how right Sai Baba was. I first had to have the experiences that my life had lacked. Otherwise, my spiritual progress would have been retarded. Now it would be easier to let go without holding on and wind up the engagements that had bound me for over thirty years.

Now I felt that it was time, that I was ready to take this important step, to take farewell of the material world which until now had engaged my thoughts and daily actions. I felt sure that I would not miss my former life. I felt a sense of relief and correctness to begin to wind up my business affairs here. To a great extent my life had been governed by materialism until now.

Ten years have now passed since I made this irrevocable decision. My initial feelings in regards to its correctness have borne fruit. I had not been ready earlier, but now the dream and yearning that had been with me since my youth could at last start to be carried into effect. Hereafter I would be able to devote all my time and power to my spiritual development and try to serve God in my fellow-creatures. God had heard my prayer to be led to a spiritually enlightened master who would be willing to accept me as his disciple. My prayer had been granted beyond all expectations when I met Sai Baba.

During the time that has passed since this transformation I have never for a single day, never for a single minute, missed my previous way of living. I have been very happy to be able to fully devote myself to carrying into effect my dream, my wish to live a calm, meditative life, with a hope to find the answers to the questions that had engaged me so strongly and marked my life.

Now I concentrated my energy on finding answers to man's eternal questions. I felt intuitively that the goal of my yearning one day would become reality. I would not fail in what I now experienced as my mission in life. I wanted to find answers to the questions of life, the Truth. Through Sai Baba's love and grace the mist began to be dispersed and the light within to shine brighter and clearer. I began to understand that the God I had yearned for was my real inner Self, that the God of creation in reality was within me, that we are One.

What did the material world mean in comparison with the spiritual world that now began to be opened for me? My new life was entirely incomparable with all that I had earlier experienced. I had myself chosen and created a world that largely had occupied my time and energy for so many years. I had undertaken duties and responsibilities which I had not been able or did not wish to withdraw from, and it had been important for me to fulfil this part of my life. Now there was nothing standing in my way any longer. My wife was as happy as I to have learnt to know Sai Baba. She was prepared any time, as soon as possible, to return to India, to Sai Baba.

In the middle of March 1980 we left Stockholm, and the whole journey was much easier this time. It was in no way as full of hardships as the previous one. We felt also happy that ashram life would not now be entirely strange. In Bangalore we took a taxi to the hotel where we had stayed previously. On arrival we came across a few Sai-devotees in the lobby, who informed us that Sai Baba now was staying in Brindavan, His ashram in Whitefield about 15 miles outside of Bangalore. This was indeed a pleasant surprise, and there was no question that we would later in the afternoon that same day take a taxi to Whitefield for Sai Baba's darshan. To have a rest after the journey was something that could wait. Soon after four o'clock we entered the ashram gates.

Brindavan was somewhat different from Prasanthi Nilayam. As one entered the main gateway, in the middle of an open space, there was a large leafy tree. Under it was an area paved with concrete, with a roof which protected devotees against the hot sun. Those who came in good time found room under the shady roof. We had to wait over an hour before Sai Baba was visible in the gateway to His private compound. It was a deep feeling of happiness to see Him again! When Sai Baba went round the platform area and gave His darshan we experienced again the strong vibrations of His divine radiation of love and light. Peace and happiness spread in our hearts, we felt that we had come home.

After darshan I met Sisko at the ashram gate and we went to have a cup of tea in one of the many primitive huts that spring up on the roadside outside the ashram, as soon as Sai Baba comes for a stay in Brindavan. After a short talk with a few Sai-friends we took a taxi to return to Bangalore. The traffic was now heavier and it took a whole hour to reach the hotel. We were rather tired by the time we reached our room and had a quick bath to remove the dust from the journey. We had a simple meal in the room and then went early to bed. We fell asleep happy to again be near Sai Baba.

In Brindavan, Whitefield

The climate in Bangalore is one of the best in India. It is unusual that the temperature rises over 30-35°C, and to this we had no objection. It was still tolerable for Northerners like ourselves. It was pleasantly cool when we descended the hotel stairs in the morning to the waiting taxi. We arrived in Whitefield in time for darshan and found our seats under the shelter in the temple grounds.

Sai Baba came. He saw me and gave me a smile of recognition. A little later He came up to me, asked when I had arrived and invited me to come in for an interview. This was indeed more than I had dared to hope, that He so immediately after our arrival would give us an interview.

I rose and began to walk towards the mandir. Sisko saw what I was doing, understood and did the same. During our previous visit we had learnt that if Sai Baba calls in one spouse, the invitation is also valid for the other partner.

There was no difference between the procedure here and that in Prasanthi Nilayam. One sits outside, and waits until Sai Baba has finished darshan and asks one to enter the interview room. Here this room was a little larger than the one in Puttaparthi, but when all had been seated on the floor, it was full. I was given a chair to sit next to Sai Baba.

When Sai Baba sat in His armchair He addressed me saying, "Very happy to see you." The happiness was indeed mutual, I could assure Him. Then He said, "Three times I have visited you in your home in Sweden, when you were sitting in meditation, and each time you twitched. Why?" I explained that maybe it was because I was not used to an Avatar suddenly coming to visit me when I was meditating, and that the surprise brought about the intense reaction. "When you meditate and have been out of body consciousness it also happens that you twitch when returning. I shall teach you to control this." And further, "Sometimes, when you have been out of body consciousness, you have been here with Me." Yes, to my happiness this I had also experienced. I had had Sai Baba's darshan without having been bodily present.

Then Sai Baba said, "I want to talk with you after evening darshan," and I understood that He meant only me. Sisko had also understood it so. Sai Baba materialized vibhuti for me and asked how it was with the cramps in my legs. I could answer that until now they had not bothered me. "Don't worry, I shall give you divine medicine." Then He asked Sisko how she was and how it was with our son. She answered that she was well and that everything also was fine with our son. She stated that she was very happy and grateful for again being with Him. "Yes, yes, I know. Very happy."

For several of the devotees present Sai Baba materialized vibhuti before He started to speak to us. He spoke about the importance of living in love, filling our lives with love, conquering our ego and every day spending some moments in stillness, prayer and meditation, thinking that God is within us. A few devotees told Him how difficult it was for them to concentrate their thoughts during meditation. "Yes, I know, monkey-mind!"

Sisko asked if Sai Baba would help her to learn to meditate, to which He said, "I shall give you a japamala (an Indian rosary with 108 beads). You just do your japa." He let His hand circulate in the air before Sisko's eyes. There hung the beautiful japamala in His hand. He showed Sisko how she should let it glide, bead after bead, over her fingers while repeating a holy mantra, one of the Names of God. Sisko had to show Him that she could handle the japamala in a proper way, and when satisfied Sai Baba hung it around her neck. Through repetition of a mantra one calms down one's mind and gradually develops one-pointed concentration. Sisko was deeply grateful for this divine gift. The interview was over and Sai Baba took farewell saying to me, "I shall see you later."

When we went out and walked towards the ashram gate we met Richard LeVan, a very sympathetic American we had come to know in Puttaparthi. In his company was a young man, Dean, from Vermont in Northern U.S.A. We went together to a refreshment hut and had a pleasant and profitable talk over a cup of tea. Richard had stayed in India during the time we had been in Sweden, and before we parted he asked if they could come for a short visit in the afternoon. They were very welcome. Whereupon we entered our taxi and drove to the hotel in Bangalore.

I kept wondering what it could be Sai Baba wanted to discuss with me in private. After lunch I sat down and took out my diary notes. The first time I had met Sai Baba I had started to make diary notes of the most memorable details of what Sai Baba said and did during our interviews and meetings. I thought it could be interesting some time in the future to be able to look back, and refresh the memory of all that had happened in and around Sai Baba's presence. At that time I could not foresee that all the richness of events that Sai Baba would let me experience one day would result in the book I'm now writing!

In the afternoon Richard and Dean arrived as planned. Over a cup of tea we resumed the talk we had begun in Brindavan. Richard told a little of what had happened during our absence. Dean was soon to return home and was sad about not having been called for an interview by Sai Baba. Without any reflection I said spontaneously, "Don't worry, you will have an interview. Wait for me tomorrow morning at the ashram gate and come then and sit beside me."

Later the same evening, when I sat in my evening meditation, I concentrated on Sai Baba and could feel His scent in the room. I prayed, "Dear Sai Baba, give me great happiness and let young Dean, who tomorrow will sit on my right hand side, have an interview. It would mean so much to him and he would be more than happy if You in Your divine love and grace would give him this blessing before he has to go home to the U.S.A. tomorrow." Afterwards I felt a wonderful peace within and my heart was filled with love for Sai Baba. I knew that He had heard my prayer, and in His love and grace He would let it happen.

The next day Sai Baba came up to me, looked at me in understanding, turned to Dean and asked him to go in.

Sisko, Richard and I waited together for Dean after darshan. Words in this connection are insufficient. It was not much Dean was able to say, only, "I'm so happy, so happy. A few days ago I didn't dare to believe that I would get an interview." Sai Baba's love had filled his heart, and so a happy Dean returned to the forests in Vermont accompanied by Sai Baba, who had consolidated His place in his heart.

During evening darshan Sai Baba asked me to come in for an interview. We were alone and He led me into the inner room. He started by asking in which hotel I was staying in Bangalore. When He heard that we were staying in the first-class luxury hotel Ashoka He asked how much our daily costs for hotel and taxi rides were. I estimated about 700-800 rupees including meals, and He shook His head seriously. "It is better you move out and come here. It is too expensive, and furthermore it disturbs your meditation to live there. I shall arrange a room for you here within the ashram and you can move in tomorrow."

Once again Sai Baba said that He was glad that I was back. "Later I shall give you a small house with two bedrooms, kitchen and lavatory. There you can live with your wife, here within the ashram." I was very happy about His offer, but wondered where this little house was situated, as I had not seen any like it. But Sai Baba assured me that, it was here, behind, in this private garden. For some days Sisko and I would first stay in a room in one of the ashram's guest houses. "Then you shall come with me to Puttaparthi. I shall let you know when we are to leave." Sai Baba rose, called for a volunteer and said that he should accompany me to the office where the room arrangement would be settled. With thanks and a bow to Sai Baba I followed the volunteer.

Sisko and I discussed Sai Baba's offer to come and live within the ashram. Of course, it meant great advantages, among others we wouldn't have to make the daily taxi rides to and from Bangalore. And furthermore it would be an advantage that we now, in a cooler climate compared to the main Ashram at Puttaparthi, could start becoming accustomed to life within an ashram. We had heard from devotees that it was very hot in Puttaparthi at this time, about 40-50°C at midday. How would we manage in such a sultry heat? We didn't even dare to think about it. Last time we were there was around Christmas time, the coolest time of the year, and the temperature had seldom risen to more than 35°C.

One day Sai Baba called me and asked, "Where do you have your Shirdi Baba ring I gave you last time you were here?" I explained what had happened, that I had put it on the table in the evening, as my fingers had become swollen in the heat and the ring was too tight. Next morning it had entirely disappeared. Then Sai Baba held out His hand towards me and asked, "Is it this ring?" He held the ring between His thumb and forefinger. I took a careful look at it and recognized my ring. Without doubt it was my Shirdi Baba ring that I had laid on the table in the room the evening before.

Sai Baba rose and asked me to come into the inner room, where we were alone. We sat opposite each other and I could clearly observe His every movement. He held the ring now as earlier between His fingers before my eyes. "Look here!" And then He blew on the ring - and it had gone. "You don't need it anymore," was His comment. By this gesture Sai Baba had given me a clear demonstration of how He transfers objects, when He wants to do so.

Back in the hotel in Bangalore we took the last chance to enjoy a refreshing dip in the swimming pool, before we went to bed for the last night in Bangalore, in Western comfort. Early next morning we packed our luggage and made ready for departure to Brindavan. Our ashram life was to begin!

One day I visited Professor N. Kasturi who lived in one of the small houses in the inner-compound garden. He wished to see me to discuss among other things an article I had written. We had not met before, but I was happy to make his acquaintance, as I had often heard about him. Professor Kasturi was always mentioned with great reverence and respect. Sai Baba had told me that he in future would be my teacher. Reverentially I approached his door and knocked.

Professor Kasturi was nearly 90 years old and had after being pensioned lived with Sai Baba, devoting all his time, energy and skill, for serving Him. Professor Kasturi radiated love and light as he stood in the doorway and held out his hands towards me in a welcoming gesture. Over a cup of tea he began to speak about the article I had written. It dealt partly with my first meeting with Sai Baba, and Professor Kasturi had discussed the article with Him. He was astonished at what I had written and said that my experiences with Sai Baba were extremely unusual and he found them very interesting. He wanted to publish the article in Sanathana Sarathi, the monthly journal of the Sai-Organization, which he edited. He was besides an author and carried out numerous commissions Sai Baba entrusted him with. Hundreds of articles are sent monthly to Sanathana Sarathi's office with a hope to be published. But in the first instance, for understandable reasons, space is of course made for Sai Baba's many discourses which He has given on various occasions. For Professor Kasturi and his colleagues it is therefore not easy to choose from the many contributions received, what is to be published. With the primary aim of the meeting over I bade farewell, and Professor Kasturi mentioned that he would come to Puttaparthi a little later, where we again could meet.

After a few days stay in Brindavan Sai Baba told me, "Tomorrow morning we shall go to Puttaparthi."

It had been wonderful, blessed days for us together with Sai Baba in Brindavan, in Whitefield, and now we were to leave, to accompany Him to Puttaparthi. At a fixed time the next morning we stood beside our taxi and waited for Sai Baba's white Mercedes. When He came He signed us to follow His car. The journey to Prasanthi Nilayam had begun.

Again in Puttaparthi

Mr. Kutumba Rao, Sai Baba's chief administrator for the Ashram, Prasanthi Nilayam, met us on arrival at the registration office. He advised that we were Sai Baba's guests and showed us to the flat that was at our disposal. To obtain Sai Baba's darshan we did not have to walk far in the sultry heat, as the flat was close to the mandir. I sent a prayer of gratitude to Sai Baba for His love and consideration. I remembered His words from our first visit, "I shall give you all you need for living here near me." Mr. Rao informed us also that a young volunteer, Panderenga, would serve us, come with our meals from Sai Baba's kitchen and take care of all other practical needs. "All as per Sai Baba's wish," as Mr. Rao expressed it, and he added, "Sai Baba's grace."

We sat down in our first home in Prasanthi Nilayam and had a refreshing cup of tea which Panderenga served. How would we ever be able to repay the divine love Sai Baba had shown us? What had we done to earn such attention and boundless love? We couldn't understand it. Sisko put this question to Professor Bhagavantam, who had come to bid us welcome. He answered, "I do not know why, but I do know that your husband has Sai Baba's grace." Mr. Rao came a little later and informed us that Sai Baba had given me a seat on the temple veranda, where I could sit on a chair in the shade, while awaiting His darshan. I was again extremely grateful for Sai Baba's consideration. It would rescue me from the heat of the open compound.

When Sai Baba came in the evening and gave His darshan He welcomed me and said that I could also sit in the mandir if I so wished. It was certainly the coolest place.

Days passed by and I was very much troubled by the oppressive heat, which in the middle of the day could rise up to

50°C. Sai Baba understood that it was difficult for me and said one day that I could go to Bangalore for a few days' rest. But I preferred to stay close to Him and hoped to become used to the heat.

I visited Professor Bhagavantam daily and received from him much valuable advice. He was very amiable and helpful, and I was happy to have such a friend to help me, to hold my hand, as they say. He led me step by step into Indian culture with its strange customs and habits, which sometimes are difficult for Westerners to understand. There happened so much around me, and it was not easy to assimilate all the new impressions I was confronted with daily. I wanted so eagerly to understand and accept the Indian way of living, but it takes time to learn and get used to.

By this time Professor Kasturi had also arrived and invited me to his discourses. He was a brilliant speaker, I forgot both time and space when listening to him. His son, Dr. Murthy, used to sit beside me. After the lectures we talked further and he explained to me what I had not understood. What had earlier been unclear now appeared in a clearer light. I learnt much, and I understood now what Sai Baba had meant when saying earlier that Professor Kasturi would be my teacher in spiritual matters.

Sometimes Sai Baba asked me to be present when He lectured to some selected students and devotees. He spoke amongst other things about how the teachings of the ancient Vedic scriptures could and should be applied and practised today in daily life. It was immensely inspiring to hear Sai Baba speak. One always came away with something to think about, the ego's influence in our life and how important it is to fight with all one's might against this 'demon' which so strongly marks our feelings, thoughts and deeds.

It is one thing to understand the significance of Sai Baba's words, this was easy, but to practise them in our daily lives is not always easy. We follow so easily the habitual tracks of our thoughts but it is difficult to break the habits of decades. We can have the will, but the ego is deep-rooted and is not easy to dislodge! We must, however, with all our power learn to control our thoughts and calm our senses in order to become masters over our ego.

How many lives had passed, and still I was standing and banging at the door to Truth! I felt now in my heart that Sai Baba through His love and grace was willing to help me with the last blows, so that the light of the soul could shine clear, purify my consciousness and let me experience and merge in God's cosmic pure consciousness.

Sai Baba had made me extremely happy when He once wrote in a letter to my home in Sweden, "I know that you search for the Truth behind the illusory world and I shall give you all the boons you ask for."

Both Sisko and I were happy to be present when Sai Baba once spoke about His next incarnation, Prema Sai Baba. On that occasion He materialized for us each a gold ring with portraits of the Hindu God Form Vishnu, Shirdi Sai Baba (His previous divine incarnation), Sathya Sai Baba and Prema Sai Baba. The picture of Prema Sai Baba was hardly discernible, as His embodiment lies in the future. We felt deep gratitude and happiness for these divine gifts. At this time I remembered the moment when I for the first time met Sai Baba and He gave me a locket showing Shirdi Baba on one side and Sai Baba on the other, saying, "You have lived very close to Me in an earlier incarnation." Now I experienced this new gift as a hopeful sign that I would be allowed to be reborn, to live close to and serve Prema Sai in my next incarnation through God's grace.

Not until we have conquered our ego and unselfishly can serve God in love are we worthy to be called devotees. We must in the true meaning of the word become One with God in all living creatures. Sai Baba made me conscious that my real inner nature is divine, but I knew also that I still have a long way to go before God in His grace can give me what I inwardly yearn for. My goal is God realization with all the divine qualities that are associated with God incarnated in human shape, like our model Sai Baba.

I pray that the divine voice of conscience shall appear clear and clean and lead me step by step away from the world of ego and illusion, that God's love and grace shall guide me, cleanse my consciousness and let me experience the merger in the true essence of divine cosmic Oneness. The significance of Sai Baba's words, "Serving hands are holier than lips that pray," is living reality. It is the way to enclose all living beings in God's love and light and serve Him in the unity of the divine creation.

One day Sai Baba called me and told that we should go to His ashram in Ooty in the Nilgiri Mountains. The climate there is cool and pleasant and would certainly do me good. We had been in Puttaparthi about three weeks when I received this happy news. "In Ooty I can give you much more time, as only a few will accompany me." Sai Baba told me also in which hotel Sisko and I should stay, and how long a time He planned to stay there. Then He lifted a forefinger towards me and warned, "But you shall not mention this journey to anybody." Sisko and I were looking forward to this journey full of happy expectations.

That same evening I visited Professor Bhagavantam, who told me that Sai Baba had asked him, "How is it with your friend from Sweden?" Professor Bhagavantam was also to come to Ooty, and the happiness in our both accompanying Sai Baba was mutual. We both laughed when he told what Sai Baba had asked him! Sometimes Sai Baba confuses us by pretending that He does not know anything. But nevertheless He knows more about us than we ourselves do. He behaves in a human way so that humanity shall feel kinship with Him. He is one hundred percent God and one hundred percent man.

In Ooty with Sai Baba

Among all the schools and universities which Sai Baba has founded and administers in India there is also a primary school, Vidya Vihar. It is beautifully situated in the Nilgiri Hills on the outskirts of the small town Ooty, the popular name for Ootacamund. Here one meets horses freely strolling around the streets, instead of the usual holy cows. A mountain lake on the outskirts of the town also contributes to the idyllic atmosphere the visitor experiences. The geographical location of the town in the mountains, makes the air cool and fresh at this time of the year, and temperatures between 25-30°C reminded us of the nicest Swedish summer.

To this wonderful place Sai Baba invited a few of His devotees to accompany Him, among them Sisko and me. We were very happy and grateful for this. It was April 1980, and we were to stay one week in Ooty. Sai Baba's words that He would have more time for us here increased our expectations further at the prospect of this, our first journey in divine company. The ride by car took almost a whole day, and in the evening we arrived at the hotel on the outskirts of the town.

Our driver was to stay and be at our disposal during the week here, and next morning we drove to Sai Baba's school and ashram on the other side of the town, a little way up on the mountain slope. Also here Sai Baba gave His darshan twice a day, to bless the local population and to their great happiness. They gathered around Sai Baba in great enthusiastic crowds.

Sisko has always been very fond of wandering in the open air enjoying nature, and she made it a habit to walk from the hotel to the ashram. In the morning she experienced the sun rise in the still, cool night air, when the town was awaking and the streets were swept clean. In the afternoon she walked through the rural crowd of business life. And then came the steep rise to the ashram, which made her a somewhat unusual sight, a

Westerner who preferred not to use a car and instead endured this hardship.

Sai Baba, who sees and knows everything, asked Sisko one day why she was walking and did not accompany her husband by car. She had answered truthfully, that she was very fond of walking and, "It is so beautiful here in Ooty." At the same time she handed Sai Baba some small wild flowers she had picked for Him on the roadside. He received them with a smile saying, "Very good, very good." After our week with Sai Baba in Ooty Sisko refers to this place as her Shangri La.

One evening the school children offered us all an unforgettable theatre performance. Under the guidance and divine inspiration of Sai Baba their acting was of the highest artistic class. The theme of their performance was built on the holy teachings of the Vedic scriptures, emphasising that the well known Hindu Gods also possessed a warm human sense of humour besides carrying out the burden of maintaining order in the entire cosmos, and guiding the development of mankind. This was a pleasant surprise to experience. We were all entirely touched by the capability of these small divine actors to give shape and life to the revered Gods.

During the performance there was intensive photographing and videotaping taking place. I wished that I had also brought a camera to capture some unforgettable pictures to take home. I made an attempt to order some pictures from a photographer, but to my disappointment he never sent me any.

I remembered how Professor Kasturi described in one of his books how one of Sai Baba's students had difficulties in giving up his habit of smoking. He had promised Sai Baba to not smoke anymore. One morning Sai Baba asked the student how it was with his smoking. The young man answered bravely, "No, Swami! I do not smoke anymore!"

Sai Baba replied, "No! You don't smoke anymore?" "No, Swami!" was the answer. A movement of the divine hand, and a photograph was created, showing this young student standing behind a corner of the school hostel- smoking a cigarette! Sai Baba handed over the picture to the student who felt deeply ashamed, both for having smoked, and for having told a lie. The student had forgot that it was Sai Baba who stood before him and had asked him - Sai Baba the omniscient, the omnipresent.

My thoughts and prayers went to Sai Baba. "Dear Swami, please be so kind to give me a few photos. You don't need any camera to take pictures with." A short time afterwards I received from Sai Baba several fine photos, among them one where He is standing between Sisko and me. On these occasions a photographer had taken the pictures, but later on I received a photograph where Sai Baba and I are sitting together, but no photographer had been present. I shall later on tell about this event.

One evening after darshan Sai Baba invited into the big interview room about twenty selected men and a number of His students from Brindavan, who had been happy enough to accompany Him on this trip. Sisko and I were also invited. Sai Baba made me sit beside Him and Sisko sat on my other side.

I expected that Sai Baba would give us a divine lecture, when He quite surprisingly addressed me. He asked me to tell about my meditation, my spiritual practices and the visions He had given me when I in the stillness of meditation had been sunk in yogic trance, outside body consciousness. "You have many times been outside your body, together with Me," He revealed.

I was a little shocked at the entirely unexpected and surprising request, as I was in no way prepared. In any case, I tried to collect my thoughts and told about my meditation habits, what it had meant for me and how my meditation had reached greater depths and a higher dimension under Sai Baba's divine guidance. I tried also to tell about the visions Sai Baba had given me, but in a rather abrupt way I then finished, turned to Sai Baba and asked, "Is it good now, can I go?" If there is anything that can astonish Sai Baba, I think that my words did astonish Him. They were at least surprising for the listeners who were present. I had been entirely unprepared for this task and felt great disappointment at not being able to tell about my experiences as completely and correctly as I had wished to do. The foreign language made it still more difficult, I could not always find the correct words.

I have never heard, and do not think that I ever shall hear, that somebody who has been invited to a meeting with Sai Baba, suddenly stood up and asked to be allowed to leave! Instead all stay as long as possible in His divine presence. There was no doubt that my behaviour made those present dumbfounded.

When Sai Baba had given me His permission to leave the room with the words, "If you so wish," I answered simply, "Yes." I went out, deeply disappointed and followed by highly astonished eyes. Later Sai Baba gave me a chance for rehabilitation, when I had the opportunity to prepare well in advance for the speech He asked me to give at the World Conference in autumn of the same year.

Here in Ooty Sai Baba had indeed been very generous towards Sisko and me. He had given us much of His time in various ways. At a group interview one morning He asked me to come earlier than usual for the evening darshan. I came, and after a short while Sai Baba called me in. We sat alone, close to each other, in the big interview room. He exchanged some personal words with me and smiled lovingly. Afterwards Sai Baba began to sing for me. I did not understand the words, as He sang in His own language, Telugu, which is quite unfamiliar to me. But, in any case, I understood. I had so many questions of a spiritual nature which I had wanted to ask Him, but had not had the opportunity. I cannot explain how it happened, but when Sai Baba sang a light was spread in my inner being and I received the answers to my unspoken questions. The answers just simply were in my consciousness.

Nothing is impossible for Sai Baba. He had lifted up my consciousness to another dimension, where I could comprehend without any explanatory words. In deep reverence I bent down and touched His divine Lotus Feet - it was difficult for me to control my inner feelings. But Sai Baba who has everything under control, said, "You must control yourself." However, He understood. I tried to collect my thoughts to thank Him, but the result was meagre. Instead we looked at each other in deep understanding, and then I left the room where this divine audience had taken place. I was in "the seventh heaven."

One day Sai Baba invited Sisko and me to a small private evening meal, only the three of us were present. During this intimate hour I had the opportunity to ask essential questions and receive answers from Sai Baba. We also each received a large-size photograph, after He had dated and signed them. In one, Sai Baba is together with His elephant, Sai Gita, who is Sisko's special friend. Sai Baba ended this wonderful evening by calling in a photographer who took a picture of the three of us standing together. It was taken with a polaroid camera, and with a loving smile Sai Baba gave it to His happy and grateful guests.

After this eventful, wonderful week in Ooty we all returned to Whitefield.

One month later Sisko and I were invited to accompany Sai Baba to Bombay. In the aeroplane I was sitting near Him, when suddenly He handed me an envelope. Somewhat astonished I held it a while in my hand, but Sai Baba said, "Open it!" I did so - and became speechless when I saw its contents. I saw, but it was hard for me to believe my eyes. In my hand I had a photograph showing Sai Baba and me on that memorable day sitting together in Ooty, when He sang for me, and He answered my many questions. And, we had been entirely, entirely alone all the time. As if to confirm my astonishment Sai Baba now said, "And no photographer was there!"

Sai Baba had answered my quiet prayer for me to have a photo of us together, yet at that time there was no camera or photographer present. And here I was sitting with one more evidence in my hand, an evidence of Sai Baba's divinity and love. There are no words to express my gratitude. I can only give Him the deep love of my heart.

I Experience the Kundalini Power

After returning from Ooty to Bangalore we stayed in the Ashoka Hotel for a few days' rest. It proved to be a wise decision.

The first morning in Brindavan Sai Baba gave no darshan. A few days later I met Professor Bhagavantam and heard that Sai Baba had been greatly preoccupied with administrative questions. As Sai Baba would also probably not give any evening darshan we decided to stay at the hotel.

In the evening I sat down for meditation, but after only a few minutes I felt a disagreeable sensation. Something was moving in my stomach. It was like a heavy ball bobbing up and down. It was not directly painful, but was however very uncomfortable, and something that I had never felt before. It started to be difficult for me to concentrate my thoughts on meditation and therefore I broke it off and lay down on my bed. This was the beginning of a nightmare-like experience.

I began to sweat abnormally. It was like a fire was let loose and raging in my body, like electric currents rushing up and down the spine. I lay in a torpid position, dozing off for awhile before awakening again shortly after. What I experienced as the electric currents increased in strength and reached right up to my head. There was a strong click, and an inferno of light spread from the head to the whole body. I thought I would be destroyed and was totally exhausted. My whole inner being was in revolt. My sight was influenced and it was difficult for me to discern the objects in the room.

My condition alternated between wakefulness and dreamlike lethargy. I had hallucinations, demons and awful, grotesque faces appeared before my inner sight, crawling reptiles of various kinds wriggled around my body. I fought to come out, to be freed from this terrible nightmare, but was entirely paralysed and couldn't do anything. At last I awoke and my head was throbbing with pain.

I am not sure how much time passed before I was again drawn into this terrible nightmare-like state. It was a dreadful experience! Sisko saw how I was suffering and wanted to call a doctor, but despite my miserable condition I declined. I had an intuitive feeling that I myself had to overcome, to fight my way through, the rage that was going on in my inner being and in my body. I had my own idea of what it was all about, what it depended on, and therefore I didn't feel it appropriate to have a doctor involved.

For quite some time during meditation I had off and on a strange feeling in the spine, like electric impulses. This feeling had not brought about any noticeable disturbance in my meditation, therefore I had not taken any serious notice of it. On several occasions, when returning to body consciousness after meditation, I had felt warm and sweaty, something that had not taken place before. But even then I did not comprehend this as a warning signal. But now I understood that these signs had a clear connection with my intensive meditation. Every day I meditated a couple of hours in the morning, some time in the middle of the day, and the evening meditation could often last 3 to 4 hours. I did not usually sleep more than 2 to 3 hours per night.

I had asked Sai Baba what these disturbances were that suddenly had begun when I meditated. He had answered, "It is the kundalini power, your chakras have opened up. Don't worry! I shall help you." At that point of time I was not very concerned about the mystic kundalini power. I trusted entirely in Sai Baba. I felt that He would lead me through the hardships I had to go through. Now I prayed to Him, "Sai Baba, please guide me through this painful struggle which I have to experience."

After once more being drawn into this painful state, I again regained consciousness of my surroundings in the hotel room. Sisko helped me to the bathroom and I took a cold shower to alleviate the fire that had ravaged through my body. She had ordered tea and cold drinks to our room, and that was exactly what I needed to refill my body fluids. I must have sweated out several litres during the last few hours. It was now two o'clock at night and Sisko was both tired and worried. She went to bed and fortunately soon fell asleep.

I remained sitting in my chair, when I again could feel symptoms of vibrating currents dashing along the spine. The last I remembered before body consciousness left me was a powerful bang, followed by an explosion of light in my head. When now relating what then happened, the picture of this experience is as clear and vivid in my memory as it was then, and is in full conformity with the notes I afterwards made.

After I had lost body consciousness I experienced how I was taken out into the cosmos on a ray of light, the like I had never seen before. The spectrum of light that surrounded me was an experience of beauty so grand that I cannot find words to describe. Fantastic is not enough. It was wonderful, so wonderfully beautiful. The entire cosmos was bathed in light, as I was floating around on the ray of light that had taken me there.

One hears people say that they have heard heavenly sweet music. I can guarantee that the tones I heard and experienced in the cosmos were indeed heavenly beautiful. I was dancing around in the cosmos on my ray of light, surrounded by divine music! I was one with the light, one with the cosmic tone-waves. Early in the morning in the mandir in Puttaparthi I could sometimes during those short hours we were sitting quiet before the light was turned on, hear the divine AUM as similar tone-waves in my inner being.

How long a time this divine vision lasted I do not know, but the dreadful nightmares that earlier had tormented me were worth suffering to gain an experience of such wonderful sweetness and beauty as this divine vision in the cosmos was.

When I returned to body consciousness I felt still how the light enlightened my whole inner being and also the room where I was sitting. I felt peace and love for God so intensively within, that I only cried and cried.

After gaining control over my feelings and senses I noticed that it was five o'clock in the morning. After having a bath and drinking several cups of tea I felt liberated and relieved. When Sisko awoke and saw me sitting peacefully in my chair, she understood that the crisis was over. Fortunately I did not have any further nightmare-like experiences , but I could still feel vibrating movements in my body, but now in a more subdued way. For several weeks afterwards I still felt them, but did not suffer, and little by little they died away.

I did not want to worry Sisko by telling her of the painful part of the experience, nor did I feel prepared, at that time, to tell about my cosmic vision. I needed time to first let everything become clear within, to study and contemplate on the experiences I had received.

Sisko thought that nevertheless we should call a doctor to examine me to see that everything was well. "Maybe you will have a relapse, so we better call a doctor." I now knew that I had regained full control and that the crisis was over, but to calm Sisko I said, "OK, let him come." There was, of course, no question of going to Whitefield that day for Sai Baba's darshan. I felt too weak for that.

After breakfast in our room Sisko phoned the reception and asked the hotel doctor to come and examine me. After a careful examination he thought that I had certainly eaten or drunk something contaminated, which often happens, especially for Westerners with sensitive stomachs, not yet used to the Indian bacteria flora. The doctor found out that there was nothing wrong with me, gave me a few pills to take morning and evening, which I never took. The real cause for calling him I didn't tell him.

The doctor wondered about our visit to India. When he heard that we were devotees of Sathya Sai Baba, had been with Him in Ooty and just arrived from there, he beamed with joy. What a fortunate coincidence - he and his whole family were also Sai-devotees!

I started to regain strength, and on the third day I felt strong enough to go to Brindavan in the evening for Sai Baba's darshan.

On our arrival a volunteer came at once up to me. It looked like he had been waiting for me. He explained that Sai Baba had already asked for me the day before, but nobody could find me. Now I should go in at once, Sai Baba wanted to see me.

Sai Baba's first question was, "Where have you been, I have been looking for you?" - "But Sai Baba, don't you know how it has been with me? I couldn't come."

Sai Baba pretended to be astonished when I told what had happened. "Yes, yes, your chakras are opening. I have guided you. Much light!" With these words He patted me on the chest. "You have been meditating too intensively. Don't worry."

Sai Baba explained that it was the kundalini power that had risen and my chakras were opened. Well, what did He mean by saying so? What does it mean that the kundalini power rises and chakras get opened?

In accord with my experience I would like to describe the kundalini power as equal to the life force in the central nervous system, which follows the spine to the nervous centre in the brain. The various so-called chakras are the nervous centres we have in the body. Through slow yoga-breathing the life force is activated and influences the various nervous centres. The increased energy activity which arises through yoga-breathing is experienced as vibrations similar to electric currents. This is what is called the rising of the kundalini power and opening of chakras, which is the consequence of intensive yoga meditation over a long time.

After one has for a long period practised meditation, spiritual exercises, the pace of breathing gets reduced to 3 to 4 times per minute It can even happen that one breathes only once per minute. Through the slow rhythmical breathing the nervous system little by little can tolerate the increased vibrations which arise as a consequence of daily practice of meditation. This slow breathing is very salutary for the nervous system, but must be slowly trained under control.

If the so-called kundalini force happens to rise too fast and uncontrolled, which often is the case in restraining one's breathing by will, this can bring about imbalance in the nervous system and also damage the organs of the body. One should therefore under no circumstances embark upon such experiments and risk one's health, without having a skilful, experienced guru who guides and oversees the practising of more advanced yoga-exercises. A warning is needed for all those who try to awaken the kundalini power by force, in the unsupervised way just mentioned.

The reason for practising this type of yoga exercise, by deliberately restraining one's breathing, is that one thinks one thereby obtains spiritual, supernatural powers, so-called siddhis. What most achieve instead are only increased ego and ruined health. In most cases the aim of spiritual development has not been realized by this method.

One who yearns for genuine spiritual development to achieve a clearer consciousness must direct one's meditation along the spiritual path which leads to an increased understanding of the true self within.

Once again I wish to thank Sai Baba for the divine experience in my cosmic vision. Sai Ram!

Warning Against False Prophets

Many who just sit still and only let their thoughts go think that they are meditating. It is not at all like that. A genuine meditation affects the whole human being in all facets. Meditation goes deep down into the inner core of a person and can make the unconscious conscious. As I have tried to explain, there are enormous powers hidden in the process of meditation, and if they are not guided in a correct way can harm a person instead of helping to achieve a richer and truer life.

Among Westerners there is a respect for Indian philosophy and knowledge, which cunning cheats in "the meditation trade" utilize for their own profit. Men and women in the West are often genuine seekers, but have not been able to find answers to their questions in the traditional religious movements. There is a belief that Indian teachings contain wisdom that demonstrates practicable ways to enlightenment. However, one doesn't know how to approach them, as the traditions and way of thinking are unfamiliar.

It is this ignorance which some deceitful exploiters have latched onto. Coolly and cynically they exploit a Westerner's sincere wish to realize the techniques and knowledge that concern one's place in infinity. As they are aware that the Westerner doesn't understand the ancient scriptures and their interpretation without long and arduous guidance of a skilful guru, they create a type of "mumbo jumbo language." They make the Westerner believe that this is the way it has to be, this is the light, the way lies open. The Westerner reads and hears this mess being expounded but still understands next to nothing - however the seeker often thinks there lies a truth hidden behind these cryptic words. When some insight dawns from the guru's "teachings," the way lies wide open to light and clarity.

These so-called gurus charge a shameless sum of money from the innocent and obedient pupils, and it happens that they can brain-wash them to an extent that they land up entirely in the clutches of the exploiter. People have committed suicide at the request of the guru or cult leader, and even collective mass suicides have occurred. The guru gets them into his power, the followers have only to obey and can be made to perform any nefarious acts. It is a repugnant shady business. It is especially the young who are most easily influenced and once exposed can be damaged irreparably.

The mission and aim of the genuine type of meditation is to create "free" individuals, in the true meaning of the word, free from desires and low thoughts which otherwise govern us. On the other hand the false meditation under the leadership of these ego-filled so-called gurus creates individuals in captivity, whose sole duty becomes to fill their bank accounts.

A genuine guru is a humble and patient person who doesn't guarantee wonders, not a human loudspeaker who promises miracles. A real guru does not cheat people out of money, whereas the fraud charges a formidable amount per hour for his conjuring tricks. A true guru assigns for the seeker a narrow and difficult path that requires much toil to reach some goals. Even when these goals are reached only more toils may be waiting, but each of these goals provides greater certainty measured by inner realizations. A false guru guarantees quick results, if he gets well paid. "Give me ten thousand Swedish crowns, and I shall make you a wise man in ten easily comprehensible lessons."

These deceivers are not easy to catch. They have resources at their disposal for advertising, printing written materials and using other marketing means, which in Western society most often replace true information. The authorities are also uncertain about these issues, as they are entirely unfamiliar with these questions and have no yardstick to use. The cheats adopt false titles and grand epithets which in the West cannot be verified.

A true guru presents the reality in its three dimensions and gives insight into the fourth. The false ones pirouette on a plane surface and declare that the scrapings thereon are the truth. These movements usually collapse when the false guru gets tired of his play or feels he is rich enough. Before that he has managed to mangle many souls, often irreparably.

So, be on your guard against these false prophets! The powers of meditation are far too strong to be handled by ruthless and greedy persons, whose sole interest is to count bank notes!

Divine Healing Power

We remained in Bangalore for a few days. Sai Baba meant for us to stay in the Ashoka Hotel to rest, and we did as before, driving to and from Brindavan for Sai Baba's darshan.

I was indeed not prepared for what was now to come. One day Sai Baba said to me, "Do not tell people about your spiritual experiences, they cannot understand and will only become envious." I answered, "I don't really understand what You mean, Sai Baba." I couldn't understand that the spiritual experiences and visions Sai Baba had given me could arouse envy in others. I had told about them only when Sai Baba Himself had asked me to do so. Sai Baba said further, "I shall help and guide you in your spiritual development. You will experience much." I was grateful and happy for the divine love and grace He always showed me, but couldn't understand why.

One morning after our arrival at Brindavan a lady came up to me and asked if I could take a look at an inflammation she had on her leg. I answered, "It must be a mistake. I'm not a doctor," and told her it would be best that she went to see one. She told me that she already had consulted and been treated by a doctor, but it hadn't helped her. "But what do you think that I could do?" Well, she had heard that I had healing powers that Sai Baba had given me. I understood now that I had to look at her leg. When I removed the bandage I found a purulent open wound. I dried it as well as I could, took the small vibhuti box that Sai Baba had given me and sprinkled vibhuti over the wound. I then bound it with a thin bandage so that fresh air could ventilate it. I gave the lady some more vibhuti, told her to clean and disinfect the wound in the evening, sprinkle a little vibhuti on it, as I had done, and then apply a thin bandage for the night. Two days later the wound was clean and a sound scab had formed. We sent a prayer of gratitude to Sai Baba. Sai Ram.

I thought to myself that it had largely been my common sense that had guided me and that vibhuti and fresh air had effectively contributed to the healing process. Sai Baba explains healing by saying, "All I do is to awaken the sick person's confidence, his own will and power to heal himself. It is My boundless love reciprocated by the devotee's intensive belief in Me that brings about the desired result."

When Sisko and I one day were alone with Sai Baba in the inner room He addressed me by saying ,"I shall give you healing power. You have only to put your hand on," and stroked me over my breast and my right arm. I was humbly grateful and happy and said that I would administer this divine gift as well as I could and in the best way try to serve God in my fellow-beings. Back home in Sweden I would think it over and find a way to practise this. However Sai Baba said, "No, no, you shall be here with Me." I made padanamaskar, touched His divine Lotus Feet, and Sisko and I took our leave.

Once back in Puttaparthi many devotees came to see me daily, hoping to receive help for their problems of the most various kinds. I did what I could, and had seldom an hour free. This took its toll, both my physical and psychic powers became more and more exhausted. One day the inevitable happened. The last visitors had left me about nine thirty in the evening and I sat a while entirely exhausted on my bed. In the night I had severe pains in my stomach and in the morning there was blood in the faeces. I had a bleeding gastric ulcer. This was a reaction one could expect as a consequence of the overwhelming burden of work I had in those months in the Ashram. When Sisko learnt of this in the morning she resolutely closed the door and said, "Now you must have rest."

That same morning I should have gone with Sai Baba for a few days' visit to Brindavan, but under these circumstances I had to cancel this journey. Sisko went and told Professor Bhagavantam about my sickness and asked him to inform Sai Baba that I was unable to accompany Him. Professor Bhagavantam soon returned with regards from Sai Baba, advising that I should stay in my room and rest until He returned. He had asked the chief physician of the ashram hospital, Dr. Alreya, to take care of me during the time He was away.

Before noon Dr. Alreya came and examined me. His diagnosis was a bleeding gastric ulcer. I knew Dr. Alreya from earlier. We used to sit side by side during Omkar in the early morning hour in the mandir and we had often talked with each other.

I took vibhuti which Sai Baba had given me. Wouldn't this and the belief in the healing power Sai Baba had awakened in me cure my gastric ulcer? Otherwise my healing powers or Sai Baba's divine medicine had little value! I had an excellent opportunity to test myself and my belief in God's healing power.

For two days I sat in deep meditation and concentrated all my power on the healing energy of light, which irradiated my sick stomach. In the morning of the second day my gastric ulcer was healed and all pains were gone. My stomach could even tolerate a little of the appropriate food Sisko had prepared.

On the third day Sai Baba returned to Prasanthi Nilayam and gave darshan in the evening. He asked Sisko how it was with me, and she could tell Him that I had recovered surprisingly fast. "Yes, yes, bleeding lasted only two days. Then it was over. Tell him to come to Me tomorrow." Sai Baba had followed the development of events and had His finger on the pulse. He guided the healing power which had cured my gastric ulcer so miraculously fast.

Sai Baba permitted me now to pass over the temple ground on the ladies' side, which was a great advantage and meant that I had a shorter distance to walk to Sai Baba in the mandir. Also He now told me that in future I should send the devotees who came to me for help either to Him or to the hospital. As it had been, I risked my own health. I should devote my time to meditation and rest.

Yes, this was how I wanted to spend my days also, but how to do it in practice! I had indeed earlier already tried to practise

Sai Baba's advice, but without great success. People just simply came, knocked at the door and stepped in. When I tried to explain to them that they must go to Sai Baba or the hospital with their problems, they said, "Sai Baba hasn't called us in for an interview, and we have to go home within a few days." This was the most common answer given. What to do under circumstances like these?

The devotees who visited me very seldom gave the least hint about their problems, but expected me to tell them. My intuition and inner sight, which in India is usually referred to as the third eye, were of great help in making a diagnosis.

We had now spent two months in India, and time seemed to be rapidly passing by. One day Sai Baba said that we would fly with Him to Bombay. He was to make His annual visit to Dharmakshetra, His magnificent Centre there. Our date of departure for Sweden suited very well the arrangements for the visit to Bombay and we were happy to make this journey together with Sai Baba before leaving India.

It was time again to bid farewell to Prasanthi Nilayam. Sisko and I were quite in agreement - we would not stay in Sweden longer than necessary before again returning to Sai Baba. After staying overnight in Bangalore we left the hotel early in the morning and arrived at the airport. There one of Sai Baba's volunteers stood waiting for us. He was in charge of arrangements for Sai Baba's journeys. Seats in the aircraft near Sai Baba were already arranged for us, we had only to check in our luggage. I received also a visiting card which I was to show to the volunteer at Dharmakshetra and which would give me access to a seat in front, near Sai Baba.

Dharmakshetra was situated a little outside the city centre, and when we arrived tens of thousands of people were already waiting for Sai Baba's darshan. Now I understood how valuable the visiting card I had been given really was. Without it we would not have had a chance to get a seat from where we could even see Sai Baba! Now a volunteer guided us to the seats Sai Baba had reserved for us.

Sai Baba came and gave His darshan for the faithful devotees who had been sitting expectantly for many hours, waiting to see Him. There was an electrifying feeling in the air, filled with love and devotion. Sai Baba spread His love and His light over the happy devotees. Following the darshan there was also singing of bhajans, which were sung with such happiness and love, that Sai bhajans were heard in the very centre of Bombay.

In Bombay we experienced two unforgettable days together with Sai Baba. After the last morning darshan a volunteer came and drove us to the temple, which was situated on a hill near the great open space where Sai Baba gives His darshan. It was the first time we visited this beautiful temple. The big hall where Sai Baba received us was extremely beautifully decorated. We were alone with Sai Baba and He offered us refreshing ice cream. He talked with us about various things that had happened during the time we had been together. It was also on this occasion Sai Baba said to me that He later would give me clear, bright views from our life together in an earlier incarnation. What divine love and grace Sai Baba again showered on us!

Sai Baba said that I should start a Sai Centre in Sweden. Also I should come back well in time for the World Conference of the Sai Organization the coming autumn in Puttaparthi, and there give a speech. I was entirely surprised by this suggestion and tried to excuse myself in various ways. I said, "I'm not used to speaking before hundreds of thousands of listeners," the estimated number of devotees to attend the Conference. I was given a loving pat on my shoulder, "You talk out of your heart." I promised to do my best.

Both Sisko and I took padanamaskar and farewell from Sai Baba, but He said, "There is no farewell. I am always with you." We both felt the truth of this in our hearts, and so it has been ever since then.

Our visit to Sai Baba was finished for this time. In the evening we left India and flew via Frankfurt home to Stockholm.

Sai Ram!

Sai Baba's Love and Grace

In Brindavan Sai Baba had given me a beautiful locket with a picture of Him sitting in a shell. He gave it saying, "I give you this locket so that you can see how I'm always sitting in your heart." Both the locket and Sai Baba's words made me very happy, but my happiness about this divine gift was not to last long. Only a few days later I bent over an electric fan that stood on the table, and then it happened. The locket was drawn into the fan blades which smashed it to pieces.

When I had picked up the broken fragments of the beautiful locket and stood with them in my hand I fell into deep despair. I lay down on the bed and asked Sai Baba to forgive me for my carelessness. The despair over what I had done affected me so strongly that when I wanted to go to the bathroom, I couldn't stand on my legs. I felt it as a treachery, and to fail God, my God. . . I tried once more to stand on my feet, but in vain. With Sisko's help I could sit up, but had neither feeling in my legs nor control over my movements. I understood that the cause for such a condition was a psychic shock after what I had just experienced.

A lady and gentleman doctor from Sai Baba's hospital came to my aid. After having examined me they couldn't understand what was wrong, and a message was therefore sent to Sai Baba, the divine doctor.

Sai Baba sent word that I be brought into the Poornachandra Auditorium where He would soon come and take care of me. I was helped there and seated on a chair, surrounded by the two doctors and Sisko. After a short while Sai Baba came and asked how it was with me. With tearful eyes I showed Him the remains of the locket and He said, "Yes, yes, the fan. Don't be sad, I shall give you another one", which later happened. Sai Baba knew what had happened without my telling Him. He gave me a loving pat on the back, stroked His hand over my legs and materialized vibhuti for me. In a moment I felt the life force again flowing through my legs. The psychic shock I had received was annulled and I was cured.

Gratitude and love for Sai Baba filled my heart to such an extent that my thoughts did not function anymore on the intellectual plane, but burst all limits of normal behaviour in His presence. I didn't think about what I did, but acted entirely spontaneously. Intoxicated by happiness I patted both the gentleman and the lady doctor. In India a man does not touch a lady in such situations, especially if unfamiliar to him!

As if that was not enough! - in the doorway a number of curious men had gathered, among them the man whom I used to engage as our driver. I called them all to come in immediately and take padanamaskar, that is bow at Sai Baba's Lotus Feet! They were most surprised and showed no reaction to my request. After I once more, in a louder voice, had repeated that they should come in, they hurried up to Sai Baba, who just stood and observed the development of events with a smile. All the men were allowed to take padanamaskar! I was so happy, so happy and wanted at this moment to share my happiness with all present. Therefore I had acted as I did, without the least reflection.

Sai Baba had seen the feelings that motivated my action. He understood my reaction, and in His love and grace He let it all happen. When I returned to my room and thought over what I had done, I was close to having a new shock! I had taken over the role that is Sai Baba's alone! It is only Sai Baba who extends this great grace to touch His divine Lotus Feet.

When I understood how wonderfully God's love can express itself, like letting such an event pass, I could only say, "Great and forgiving are You in Your divine, omniscient love! I thank You, beloved Sai Baba."

My driver Babu came later in the evening with regards from his comrades. They hadn't talked about anything else other than the incredible, the fantastic experience that had happened to them.

The happiness, the joy to have come so close to Sai Baba for the first time in their lives, and furthermore be allowed to take padanamaskar, was indescribable. They all sent their regards and thanks. I said that it was Sai Baba they ought to thank, for He in His divine love and grace had let this wonderful event happen.

I was tremendously grateful to Sai Baba for giving me so much of His precious time and divine love. During my short stay with Him He had blessed me with more personal interviews than I ever had dared to hope for. That this was unusual was confirmed by the questions people around me asked.

I can understand those who asked me if I was very sick, as Sai Baba in the first place devotes much of His time to sick persons as well as those with problems that are difficult for them to bear. An old Indian devotee asked me one day, "Are you very ill, or what is the reason that Sai Baba gives you so much attention?" I could only answer truthfully, that I in no way felt sick. Disregarding common faintness on account of the climate I was in good health and spirits.

I was also asked, "Why have you come to Sai Baba?" Again I could only answer as it was. I had come because I felt love and longing in my heart to meet and learn to know Sai Baba. I had not come to have any wishes fulfilled other than my yearning for Truth and love for God.

During this my second visit I became more and more interested in Sai Baba's social work. As a Swede, this "lies in the spine" - in our rich country we could afford to build up a comprehensive welfare system.

As I have mentioned earlier, Sai Baba has in the field of education founded many schools and colleges on all levels. He has built up several hospitals and an extensive, well functioning program for health and medical services in the countryside. Much important work is done in the slum districts in various cities and in the most distressed villages.

One can easily understand how extremely appreciated and important the free medical care is that Sai Baba offers to poor sick people. He calls together medical specialists, who voluntarily put their time and knowledge at disposal in various places and parts of the country, where the need for help is the greatest. During the World Conference in 1980 I saw several hundred doctors come to Sai Baba's Ashram, where temporary medical surgeries and operation halls had been erected. For instance a great number of eye operations were carried out, as cataract is widely spread in India. Orthopaedic operations helped many a poor person to a new mobility. Most diseases could be treated here by specialists from all over India and also foreign countries, and the after-care was carried out by volunteers who were trained in nursing. This was no isolated phenomenon, similar aid is given many times each year in different places in the country.

Valuable assistance work is carried out where the need for help is most acute, for instance during catastrophes of various kinds, which are not unusual in India. Thousands of students and devotees offer their time and energy on such occasions each year.

Sai Baba strongly emphasizes that all participate in this type of service work. He says that loving service to our fellow-beings is the best spiritual practice for us. To serve our neighbour is to serve God.

I have tried to give a brief picture of the divine, important work that the Sai Organization through its Centres, with Sai Baba's guidance and inspiration, carries out within various fields of social life all over the world. There is distress and ignorance everywhere, the need for help, especially in coping with daily life. Sai Baba's love and work embraces the whole of humanity.

Our omniscient, omnipresent Sai Baba calls for the same selfless service and spirit of self-sacrifice, that He Himself demonstrates, from the members of His organization in all countries all over the world. There are firm rules and regulations for all to follow, with modifications depending on different prevailing circumstances and special needs in each specific country. This contributes to demolishing the boundaries between nations and races - it teaches us to become conscious of the divine Oneness that unites us all. It teaches us coexistence in love.

Visit to Sai Centres in London

Returning home after more than two months' stay with Sai Baba in India, our friends understood that it was not just a sudden transient interest, when they heard with what happiness and enthusiasm we spoke about Sai Baba and our future. The time with Sai Baba had given us so enormously much of all that both Sisko and I had longed for in our inner hearts since our youth. We had a wonderful, liberating feeling the further we advanced with winding up our business affairs and withdrawing from the material world. Thus we could devote our time and energy to spiritual matters.

In the summer of 1980 Sisko and I were invited to London to visit Sai Centres there. We thought it would be interesting to study how a Sai Organization functioned in a land outside of India. We understood that these Centres had already existed in London for many years.

We were very hospitably received and saw again several devotees we had met earlier in India. There were a main Centre and five to six smaller ones in this big city. Their activities closely adhered to the rules and regulations of the Organization concerning administration and functioning of Centres. Our visit was therefore valuable and informative as a means to start a Centre in Sweden.

We had also the opportunity in London to listen to Mr Mathoor Krishnamurti, manager of the Indian Cultural Centre, Bharatiya Vidya Bhavan. He was surrounded by an aura of light and love. His deep knowledge and fascinating explanations made one really imbibe all the divine wisdom which he made clear. After the meeting Mr Krishnamurti came up to me and invited us to visit him, which we gladly did a few days later. We spent a couple of pleasant and instructive hours in his company. We were filled with much inspiration when we farewelled him and his wife.

Time passed all too quickly. There was so much we wanted to study and learn during the week we spent in London. Inspired by what I had seen and experienced, I was now to take up the preparatory work for starting a Sai Centre in Sweden, as Sai Baba had asked me to do.

During our journeys in India we had come to know many enthusiastic Sai devotees from Sweden. Sai Baba's wish that a Centre be formed in Sweden was met with great joy. It was decided that we would have our first satsang, spiritual gathering, in Omberg near Motala, where a beautifully situated tourist hotel could provide lodging for all of us. We felt Sai Baba's blessing and presence in all we did during that week. Our days were filled with various activities. Beside meetings for solving organizational questions there were discourses on the program, a film was shown about Sai Baba and bhajans were sung morning and evening. There was also time for daily rest and meditation as well as excursions in the beautiful surroundings.

After our work was finished, we were all happy to record that the first Sai Centre had been established in Sweden. We all felt great gratitude and happiness that a uniting organ for spreading Sai Baba's divine message of love was built in Scandinavia.

At that time there were not more than about fifty Sai devotees in Sweden, but the number was growing rapidly. When we were in India with Sai Baba, during Christmas in 1980, that is about only half a year later, we learnt from newly arrived Swedish devotees there were about two hundred members.

In India I came to know several Danish devotees who wished to start a Centre in Denmark. A few months later, during spring time, their wish was fulfilled. Before the end of the year there were three Sai Centres in Sweden and two in Denmark, officially registered in India, with a fourth Centre being established in Sweden. The number of devotees in Scandinavia had increased with the speed of an avalanche, and it was not unusual for groups of between thirty to forty Scandinavians to visit Sai Baba.

We had decided to make another trip to India, our third such. There were many practical considerations to be thought over before we could depart Sweden and go to Sai Baba. The Swedish summer soon changed into autumn. One could already catch glimpses of the beautiful autumn colours in nature. We completed all arrangements as well as possible to enable us to stay with Sai Baba for a period of four to five months.

The Third World Conference of the Sai Organization

In the middle of September 1980 we left Sweden for our third visit to Sai Baba and landed safely and happily in Bangalore. We stayed there a few days to rest and to obtain provisions before the taxi ride to Puttaparthi.

We departed early in the morning eager to see Sai Baba again, in just a few hours time. Approximately three kilometres from Puttaparthi we suddenly saw Sai Baba's white Mercedes coming towards us. What did this mean? Was Sai Baba leaving Puttaparthi just as we were arriving? But, the Mercedes stopped beside our taxi. Sai Baba opened His door and we hurried up to Him. He took my outstretched hands and said, "Very happy to see you both." "But, Sai Baba," I stammered, "are You leaving Puttaparthi?" "No, no, I came only to meet you." - Sisko and I were deeply moved by Sai Baba's love, to come especially to meet and welcome us!

Sai Baba said, "I shall return with you." His driver turned the car and we followed it. Soon we were in Puttaparthi. Sai Baba took the turn towards the mandir and gave His darshan to the waiting devotees. We stopped outside the registration office.

Mr. Kutumba Rao, the chief administrator of the Ashram, came and bade us welcome. Once again Sai Baba had allocated a comfortable flat for us. Mr Rao informed us that preparations for the World Conference were well under way and that he would help us with anything we needed. We were very grateful for the hospitality Sai Baba again showed us.

I went to see Professor Bhagavantam, who confirmed that Sai Baba had awaited us. I then told about the divine reception that had welcomed us on our way. "I know! Go now and have a rest. Come then to Sai Baba's evening darshan." We had lunch and took a short rest before the time for darshan.

Sai Baba came up to where I was sitting on the mandir veranda and asked if everything was well. I answered, "Our arrival was prepared with divine love and consideration. My wife and I are very glad to be here again with You."

"Yes, I know," He replied. Then I received a loving pat on my head and on He went. After darshan we stayed and joined in the bhajans. Our first happy day with Sai Baba soon came to an end.

Preparations for the coming World Conference in November could be observed all over the Ashram. Among other work there was construction on a large round building, consisting of four floors of residential units, in progress. It was situated on a small rise on the outskirts of the old ashram area, with a beautiful view in all directions. The units were to be ready for moving in before the World Conference.

Artists and sculptors were busy with the decoration work in the huge Poornachandra Auditorium, with seating room for over twenty thousand persons. Here a great part of the festivities, including Baba's discourses, were to take place. They were transforming the stage area with several fine plaster reliefs portraying key scenes from some of the major religions. The entire auditorium complex is unique with its sculptured columns placed up and down the length of the building, supporting a space framed roof across the width. As a result there are no internal columns to obstruct the audience's view of the stage. It has been recorded that this is the largest auditorium of its kind in Asia, and Sai Baba played a key role in the design of the space frame. The engineers at first said it was impossible, but Sai Baba showed them the way!

The World Conference in 1980 was the third of its kind. These are being held every fifth year in Puttaparthi, around the time of Sai Baba's birthday on November 23rd. Sai Baba had arranged the Conference to coincide with His birthday, so that devotees from all over the world would have the chance to participate in both these functions with only one journey to Puttaparthi. It was estimated that some five-to-six hundred thousand devotees would gather in Puttaparthi during this period.

An astronomic number, it seemed to me. It was something indescribable, incomprehensible for a Westerner, to once in a life-time be present at and have the chance to experience such a fantastic manifestation of devotion. Increasing thousands of devotees now began to arrive every day at the Ashram, especially nearer the great jubilee day.

One day I was with Sai Baba in the Poornachandra Auditorium. We went around together and looked at all the beautiful, artistically decorated symbols of the various religions. We went up on the dais and looked out over the enormous hall. Sai Baba said, "Here you will stand and speak, and here I shall sit and listen to you." By His words I was now reminded what was in store for me. I felt butterflies in my stomach when I thought that here in this hall at least twenty thousand people would sit and listen, and that outside there would be hundreds of thousands of devotees, who, through loud-speakers and television, could follow what was happening inside.

I said, "Sai Baba, I'm not sure that I shall be able to manage to speak before all the hundreds of thousands of devotees who will sit all around and listen."

Sai Baba answered, "I know what you will say. You will speak out of your heart, it will be fine."

Professor Bhagavantam showed that he really was a true friend when one day he asked if he could visit me and, if I so wished, I could rehearse my speech in his presence. I thanked him for his kind consideration. It would give me a needed feeling of confidence. Professor Bhagavantam had my highest respect.

The round house was now ready. Some days before Sai Baba was to inaugurate this impressive building Mr Rao explained that Sai Baba had given me a flat with two interconnecting bedrooms, a kitchen and a bathroom. I was given the freedom to choose any of the units to my liking! This was both surprising and very pleasant news, which I could not have dreamt of. Sisko and I were most grateful and chose a beautiful flat, which let in plenty of light, on the second floor, towards the north. Afterwards I went to Sai Baba and thanked Him for the divine love and grace He again had showed Sisko and me. "Well, there you can live comfortably," was Sai Baba's comment.

The next day Sisko and I went to Bangalore to buy furniture and a refrigerator. Late in the evening we were back in Prasanthi Nilayam, tired but happy for our new home that Sai Baba had given us and which we now were to fit out. A few days before the beginning of the World Conference we moved into our new home.

And then the great festivities started. Sai Baba opened the World Conference by welcoming all devotees. They had come from all corners of the world, from near and far, from North and South, East and West. All the hundreds of thousands who were here represented various cultural and religious beliefs, but all were united through Sai Baba's divine love.

The first days were mainly taken up by speeches dealing with organizational questions on both international and local levels. When these questions were dealt with and guidelines for the future work within the Organization were established, the jubilee festivities began with official speeches by delegates and persons, who were personally invited to do so by Sai Baba. Now the hour had come for me to participate. Professor Bhagavantam had asked me beforehand if I would like to begin this part of the program.

I went up to Sai Baba, took padanamaskar and received His blessing. After the first sentences the stage-fright vanished, and I thought it all went off quite well. Afterwards several kind devotees came up to me, clasped my hands and told me my speech had been engaging. Among these was, of course, my friend Professor Bhagavantam. Relieved and relaxed I took my seat to listen to the next speaker. One illuminating speech succeeded another.

At the conclusion of each day there were various music and theatre performances by both professional artists and Sai Baba's own pupils, from the youngest to the oldest. Every day was filled with interesting moments. The highlights were, of course, Sai Baba's discourses. Sai Baba's divine boundless love and sympathy beamed towards us when He blessed His devotees in the

Poornachandra Auditorium. His blessing also reached out through loud-speakers to all the hundreds of thousands who were sitting outside.

The festivities reached their peak with the celebration of Sai Baba's Birthday on November 23rd. A representative of each country was then to offer a garland of flowers and also have the good fortune to touch His divine Lotus Feet. I was one of those fortunate. Sai Baba was extolled in speeches, followed by orchestral music performed by His College students and some renowned musicians. But above all, homage was paid to Sai Baba by all His devotees' love, devotion and gratitude. Sai Baba says, "You celebrate My birthday that day when you became conscious of My presence in your heart."

The World Conference and Sai Baba's Birthday celebration was finished with a magnificent firework display. The memory of all the experiences during this gigantic festival still live in my mind, when now sitting and writing. I cannot even try to do justice to the magnificent settings and the vibrating spiritual light, which permeated the air in Prasanthi Nilayam. Sai Baba said that the Conference had been visited by more than five hundred thousand devotees, and the organization behind all was indeed impressive. For one thing, the magnitude of Sai Baba's heart was such that all those present were fed for several days without having to pay anything.

In Bangalore After the World Conference

To relieve the pressure in Prasanthi Nilayam and to encourage the innumerable devotees to return home, Sai Baba told me a week after the festive days had ended that He would go to Whitefield for a few days and from there to Madras. Sisko and I were welcome to follow Him on this journey.

It was a wonderful relief to enter the ashram compound in Brindavan. The air was cool and refreshing - the climate in the Bangalore district is indeed pleasant, very much like Swedish midsummer at its best.

The Shilton Hotel in Bangalore was well-known and frequently visited by Western Sai devotees. During our stay in the city we had lunch there now and then and had come to know the owner, Mr. Mushtaq Noorani. One day when visiting the hotel Mr.. Noorani came and greeted us. He wondered how long we would stay in Bangalore and, to our complete surprise, invited us to be his guests in his villa outside the city. He insisted that it would only be a pleasure for him if we accepted. We understood that it came out of an honest heart and didn't want to hurt him, so we accepted his kind invitation.

After lunch Mr. Noorani's driver picked us up and took us to his home where our host was already waiting for us. It was a beautiful, spacious villa, and a luxurious guestroom with private bathroom was at our disposal. We had afternoon tea together and were introduced to the cook, who would take care of us together with the maid. Mr. Noorani declared also his wish that we as his guests would have our meals in his house and that the driver would take us daily to and from Brindavan. Once again we were entirely taken aback by his generosity!

Mr. Noorani lived in the villa with his two children of around ten years of age. He was a Muslim. In the evening after having had dinner together, he explained that he had heard about my close relationship with Sai Baba and hoped I would tell him about it. Those evenings were pleasant, sitting with Mr.. Noorani and relating what we knew about Sai Baba!

After two days as guests and having been taken very well care of in Mr. Noorani's hospitable house, Sai Baba approached me one morning in the compound and asked where I was staying. I understood that He knew very well where we were staying, but asked anyway, to hear what I had to say. I told Him that Mr. Noorani, the owner of the Shilton Hotel in Bangalore, had very generously invited us to be his guests in his home during our time there, and that I could not decline his hospitality. I said also that I had found Mr. Noorani to be a good man and that he was eager to hear me tell about Sai Baba. I continued, "Sai Baba, tomorrow I can bring him here, so You can meet and learn to know him." - I noticed that my words seemed to surprise Sai Baba. He said, "Yes, yes," and left to give darshan to His devotees who were waiting.

In the evening I told Mr. Noorani that he should accompany us next morning to Brindavan, Sai Baba wanted to meet him. If Sai Baba, in the morning, seemed surprised at my words, it was nothing in comparison with Mr. Noorani's reaction. He wondered, of course, why Sai Baba wanted to meet him, and I explained in short that I had asked Sai Baba to let him come with me to Him.

In Brindavan there was great astonishment among Western devotees, who knew Mr. Noorani, when they saw who was walking by my side towards the interview room! And also in the interview room eyes were opened wide in astonishment when they saw who accompanied me this morning. Mr. Noorani sat down on the floor beside me, and a few minutes later Sai Baba came in. He came and exchanged greetings with Mr. Noorani, who expressed his happiness that we were his personal guests. Sai Baba asked then what Mr. Noorani wished, but he could not give any answer. Sai Baba took my hand and showed him the ring on my finger, which He had given me. "I want to give you a photograph of this ring," Sai Baba said. Then He stretched out His hand, a few circular movements, and there was a photograph of my ring. Sai Baba gave this and also vibhuti to the astonished Mr. Noorani, who thanked Him for having received him and given him His blessings.

Later when coming out into the compound several devotees approached us wondering about Mr. Noorani's presence and also that Sai Baba had given him darshan. Mr. Noorani showed the photo Sai Baba had materialized for him and said, "It was Mr.. Curth who wanted that I should meet Sai Baba, and Sai Baba had agreed."

We drove to the hotel where Mr. Noorani entertained us to lunch. Here still more devotees came and wanted to know how it had come about that he had been with me to Sai Baba. They knew he was no Sai devotee, and had never tried to go to Brindavan to obtain Sai Baba's darshan. Mr. Noorani tried again to explain how things had happened. We had no chance to sit and have our lunch in peace, the curiosity was too obtrusive.

In any case Sai Baba had nothing against Sisko and me staying as guests in Mr. Noorani's home for the duration of our stay in Bangalore. This was soon at an end, and Sai Baba said that we should travel with Him to Madras to visit His ashram, Sundaram. We took farewell of Mr. Noorani, his two very nice children, the capable cook and the helpful maid. We couldn't but give them all our sincere and hearty thanks for the hospitality and kind consideration we had enjoyed in their beautiful home.

In Madras with Sai Baba

To travel around in India with Sai Baba and visit His various ashrams is indeed very interesting and enlightening. At the time we visited Madras there was a large conference going on and all the big hotels were fully occupied. I talked with Professor Bhagavantam and wondered what we should do, as the flight company had not been able to make an advance booking for us. "Don't worry, Sai Baba will see to it," he assured us. No, we were not worried, but understood that the hotel question would be solved in some way or other and departed therefore confidently.

Sai Baba and His closest service personnel lived within the ashram Sundaram. Sundaram is not an ashram where devotees can stay like Prasanthi Nilayam and Brindavan. In front of the mandir there is a spacious open area where devotees gather for Sai Baba's darshan.

Sai Baba had arrived in Madras on an earlier flight in the afternoon, whilst we travelled on a later evening flight. While standing waiting for our luggage a volunteer approached and asked if I was Mr. Curth from Sweden. He took care of our luggage and led us to a car waiting outside. We were driven to a first-class hotel where reservation had been made for us - Sai Baba had arranged everything. We were asked to be at Sundaram next morning nine o'clock at the latest.

We entered through the gateway to Sundaram in good time. Sundaram means beauty in Sanskrit. The great temple building was certainly very beautiful - living up to its name! We were at once taken care of by volunteers, who showed us to our respective seats. Here, like everywhere else when Sai Baba visits and grants darshan, innumerable devotees are gathered, and it can be difficult to find one's way through the crowd. I was happy to have a seat under an erected sun shelter - the sun already stood high in the sky and it would become very hot later in the afternoon.

Some time after we had been seated Sai Baba came to give His darshan. He walked around both the gentlemen's and ladies' sides, greeting His faithful devotees who had been sitting and waiting for Him for several hours. The bhajans were programmed to start at eleven o'clock. Everything took a longer time than we had expected and our driver was impatiently waiting for us when we at last found him in the throng of people and taxi cabs.

We had lunch and took some rest before the driver came later in the afternoon to take us back to Sundaram. Now the number of devotees waiting outside the gateway was even larger - they stood there hoping to see Sai Baba pass, and it took time to advance the short distance we had to walk. It is difficult for a Westerner to comprehend such sacrificing, patient devotion.

We had, of course, already become a little used to the oppressive heat in India, but I was happily surprised when a volunteer asked me if I wanted to go and sit in the cool mandir. When I entered, there were already about 30 persons, men and women, quietly sitting and waiting. They were all especially called in by Sai Baba for a private interview before darshan. He spoke a while with each one before He went out to give darshan to those faithfully waiting.

Outside the mandir Professor Bhagavantam stood waiting for me. We were seated together in the shade in front of a constructed platform, where the leader of the Madras Sai Organization was to give a welcome speech for Sai Baba. As in Bombay, one could feel a special enthusiasm and devotion here. Bhajans concluded the first day of Sai Baba's two days' stay in Madras.

It had been an interesting but hot and tiresome day. After dinner Sisko and I took a quiet walk in the hotel surroundings before we retired early to bed. We were full of expectation for another eventful day.

Sai Baba had organized His visit in Madras to take place over a weekend so that many officials of high station, within both the state and public administration as well as the educational system, were free and could participate. Among the speakers this day, besides of course Sai Baba, were also representatives of the Madras University.

That it was Sunday was indeed clearly noticeable. The enormous hall where this event took place was more than filled to capacity, and also the passage ways and the garden around the building were crowded with devotees.

When Sai Baba arrived He gave darshan before He was seated on the dais in the middle of the hall, and then the first speaker approached the platform. To sit for several hours listening to various discourses in that heat was strenuous. To maintain full concentration and understand what is said in English with an Indian accent doesn't make things any easier. Fortunately Professor Bhagavantam's son, whom I already knew, was sitting beside me. He was of great help and explained anything which had been difficult for me to understand.

After a short break for lunch we had the pleasure to listen to an excellent program consisting of instrumental music and song, mainly performed by artists from Madras. Afterwards followed what all had been waiting for, Sai Baba's speech to His devotees. In the evening young people from the Madras Sai Organization gave an excellent theatre performance, which concluded Sai Baba's visit to Madras.

Early on Monday morning we took the flight back to Bangalore. Everything had passed so quickly. Our days with Sai Baba had been so intense, completely filled with sterling experiences on the spiritual as well as the cultural plane. It took a long time for us to assimilate all we had experienced in Madras.

I was astonished when a Sai devotee in Brindavan, soon after our return from Madras, asked me, "Who are you? Why does Sai Baba give you so much attention? Devotees come here from far away, from all over the whole world. They have to wait for weeks, for months, well, even for years, before Sai Baba invites them for an interview. I myself have lived near Sai Baba for many years, but have only been given a few interviews. During the short time you have been here you have had many more interviews, much more attention than most others who have lived close to Sai Baba for many years."

In his way of expressing himself I could clearly see what Sai Baba had meant when saying to me, "Many will be jealous of you."

I tried to understand this man's reaction and feelings. He was a middle-aged man who in devotion had spent many years of his life near Sai Baba. Each one has his or her own way to go in order to learn the lessons of life. To accept with humility and a contented heart what we have to go through to develop spiritually is not always easy.

I was unable to give the man a satisfactory answer. I didn't know myself and also kept asking what the reason was for Sai Baba giving me so much love. Perhaps the answer was to be searched for in my previous life, when I, as Sai Baba had said, had been living close to Him?

At this time Sai Baba had not yet given me those clear recollections of our earlier life together which He had promised me in Bombay. However I felt intuitively that the answers to the man's and my own questions lay in my relationship and nearness to Sai Baba in an earlier life.

I had come because Sai Baba had called me, and I felt that He was willing to guide my continued spiritual development. I was obsessed by yearning and love for God and a wish to experience oneness with God in my heart. Sai Baba had felt my yearning and had called me. The happiness at seeing each other again was mutual. Under Sai Baba's divine guidance I could resume the spiritual yoga practices which I had earlier carried on at His side.

Inspiring Persons I Met Near Sai Baba

God has given us different gifts. No one is worth more than anyone else. Each one has their task to fulfil, and therefore we must always make good use of our time. Sai Baba says, "Time wasted is life wasted." - Our time belongs to God.

Somebody may express his or her service to God in an obvious way, but also this can be done less obviously in serving mankind. Sai Baba says, "Service to man is service to God." Through bhakti yoga, love for God, our thoughts are purified and our heart filled with love.

In Sai Baba's Ashram I had the opportunity to meet several persons who were close to Him and who, each one in his way, contributed to my development. I am humbly grateful to Sai Baba for allowing me to get to know them.

<u>Professor N. Kasturi</u>

Professor Kasturi had been drawn to Sai Baba, when Sai Baba was a young man and has devotedly and lovingly served Him ever since. Kasturi had been a well known media personality, especially for being able to portray good humour in his radio talks and newspaper articles. To meet Professor Kasturi was also to meet a light of wisdom and love. One felt that one was standing before a great personality. Only one who has lived with love deeply rooted in his heart possesses a radiation like his.

Many books about Sai Baba have, over the passing of some forty years, left Professor Kasturi's desk. Numerous are the discourses with which in an incomparable way he has described, translated and illumined the Avatar Sri Sathya Sai Baba's message of love, His life and work. Sai Baba granted Professor Kasturi the rare privilege of being His biographer as well as the editor of the monthly Ashram publication, Sanathana Sarathi.

On some occasions I had the pleasure to listen to Professor Kasturi's lectures. He indeed possessed the gift to spellbind his listeners, to give life to words. A highly gifted, God-devoted person, who had the capacity to give his listeners lasting impressions about what they heard. His warm humour made his books and discourses an unforgettable experience for us all.

What a source of inspiration it was to listen to a man who through the grace of God had received such abundant divine gifts! How well Professor Kasturi had managed to use them! How inspiring it was to listen when he spoke of Sai Baba's message of love to humanity! For me the memory of Professor Kasturi stands out as a model of humility and selfless service to God.

In August 1987, at the age of ninety, Professor Kasturi left his body in the presence of Sai Baba in Puttaparthi. I'm grateful for the great privilege and pleasure to have had personal contact with him.

<u>Dr. S. Bhagavantam</u>

Dr. Bhagavantam became a close friend of mine, whom I visited almost every day and had a profitable talk with. He was full of love and understanding and had always, despite his great burden of work, some free time for me and my many questions.

For a stranger it is not easy to understand all the spiritual richness the Indian culture has over thousands of years brought forth. This richness has marked daily life in India, especially that found in an ashram. Dr. Bhagavantam guided me gently and gave me many invaluable lessons. It was very inspiring to listen to a man who possessed so much knowledge and wisdom in so many fields as Dr. Bhagavantam did.

As a pensioner, after an internationally acclaimed career in the service of science as a leading physicist, Dr. Bhagavantam had retired, dropped all his fine titles, as he himself expressed it, and had lived for several years in the Ashram in the service of Sai Baba. Many may recall Dr. Bhagavantam as one of a small core of devotees Sai Baba called upon to translate discourses from Telugu into English. From about 1965 onwards Sai Baba initiated a long term program to transform the system of education in India, with an emphasis on education in human values. Dr. Bhagavantam played a key role in its development.

A few years ago I heard that Dr. Bhagavantam, on account of sickness, had left Puttaparthi to live with his children. I hope that my friend after a long, busy and distinguished working life will experience peace and happiness in the circle of his dear ones.

It is for me a great pleasure and honour to be able to present Dr. Bhagavantam's discourse on science and spirituality, delivered at the Third World Conference in 1980, in the next chapter. I received his permission for publication and can only hope that the reader will find it as interesting and informative as I do.

Dr. Bhagavantam was indeed a good teacher for his friend from Sweden, as he used to call me. I feel warm affection and gratitude for his love and great patience with me.

Professor V.K. Gokak

Professor Gokak has written many books which have been translated into several languages. He is well-known even to Western readers as an author and poet. I have had the privilege to read some of his works which have made a strong impression on me.

Having been granted a pension after a distinguished career within the Indian university system, Professor Gokak now devotes his energy and great knowledge in the management of Sai Baba's universities and schools.

When Professor Gokak one day came to me and introduced the idea that I should write a book about my spiritual experiences under Sai Baba's divine guidance, I shook my head. I had also done so earlier, when Sai Baba had asked me to come to Puttaparthi for the World Conference in the autumn of 1980 to present a speech. Both thoughts appeared equally strange to me. I thought it was outside of my experience and considered that I lacked both knowledge and capacity for carrying out either of these tasks in a satisfactory way. So I felt at that time!

Man proposes, God disposes! I did as Sai Baba had asked. I gave a speech at the World Conference. And today, in 1990, I am completing the manuscript that maybe one day will become the book Professor Gokak requested me to write. God's inspiration has ripened into action. Everything has its origin in God.

We human beings are like small puppets in the hands of God. He pulls a string, and we lift a hand. He gives us a push, and we start moving where He wills. In common parlance we say, "I was inspired to do this or that." Through inspiration God's will is expressed in our deeds.

God is the great conductor in the illusory world we are living in. It is He who directs this play and distributes the roles. God gives us the text and the words, He creates the movements. It would be wise if we learnt to realize this and thus could liberate ourselves from the illusion of this seeming reality all around us. I had myself lived in this illusory world for many years, lived on the surface without understanding what there was underneath.

"By our own efforts we can do nothing," is one of the many truths Jesus revealed during his life on Earth, as valid and true today as then, for we cannot do anything without God's grace.

Dr. John S. Hislop

During my visits to Sai Baba I had also the privilege and pleasure to learn to know Dr. Hislop.

I felt great admiration for the devoted and inspiring work he has unceasingly done for many years as the Chairperson of the Sai Organization in the United States. He has also in writings and books shared his rich experiences as a humble servant of Sai Baba. In one of his books, "Conversations with Bhagavan Sri Sathya Sai Baba," which also is translated into Swedish and is highly appreciated, Dr. Hislop puts to Sai Baba just those spiritual questions which many of us had wished to ask. Divine answers to these essential questions are here given.

I am very grateful that Dr. Hislop gave me time for instructive conversations, when I had the possibility to ask many questions of both a spiritual and organizational nature which were of importance to me. I wish Dr. Hislop all success in his devoted work in the service of Sai Baba as both Chairperson and author.

During my stay with Sai Baba I was met with much kindness and helpfulness in various forms. Many are the Sai friends I have in dear and grateful memory. Those I have mentioned are only a few of all the persons who enriched my days with Sai Baba.

Bhagavan Sri Sathya Sai Baba An Avatar of the Current Era

By Dr. S. Bhagavantam
(Formerly Scientific Adviser to the Minister of Defence, Government of India)

(I am very grateful to my friend Dr. S. Bhagavantam for having in trust given me a copy of his 1980 discourse regarding spirituality and science with the above title, with permission to have it published).

According to the traditional beliefs of India, God incarnates on Earth at times of great suffering, deterioration of moral standards and disappearance of human qualities like love and compassion. God, so incarnating and appearing in human form amongst the people, is called an "Avatar." Such an advent has for its objectives the salvation and rescue of mankind and the restoration of righteous conduct for the good of all the people of the world. Bhagavan Sri Sathya Sai Baba is an incarnation of God and was born on November 23, 1926 in the small village of Puttaparthi on the banks of the Chitravathi River in the Southern State of India, Andhra Pradesh. At the age of fourteen, He proclaimed His mission as one of establishing faith in God and fear of sin in the minds of all people, thereby leading them to the goal of brotherhood of man and fatherhood of God.

As a part of His mission, He has established schools, colleges and hospitals where the workers practise selfless service with the conviction that, "service to man is service to God." At present, He has over 30 million followers or devotees in various countries all over the world. His message has thus spread, crossing national, political and linguistic barriers and has acquired a universality in its appeal to mankind. Sathya Sai Baba is widely regarded not only as a spiritual leader but also as God incarnate in contemporary times. Unlike what is known to have happened in the past in regard to such incarnations and spiritual leaders, Sathya Sai Baba has become a legendary figure even in his life-time. In connection with the Third World Conference of the Sathya Sai Organizations, several hundreds of thousands of His devotees from all corners of the world have gathered at His abode in Puttaparthi, on the occasion of His fifty fifth birthday in November 1980. Many of them came to Him for spiritual enlightenment, for mental peace and solace and to bask in the sunshine of compassion and love which He radiates continually and in abundance. They all participate joyously in the silent revolution which is being brought about through the institutions, and individual programmes which Baba has initiated.

It is on record that when Albert Einstein, the famous scientist, was asked whether he thought that everything could ultimately be expressed in scientific terms, he replied, "Yes, that is conceivable, but it would make no sense. It would be as if one were to reproduce Beethoven's Ninth Symphony in the form of an air pressure curve." This, indeed, is very much so with all things that are beautiful, that are Divine and that give joy and bliss to the human mind as distinct from pleasure and comfort to the human body. Beauty like love and affection can only be experienced and not expounded. So also, Divinity like faith and tranquillity can only be experienced and not expounded. Yet, many people ask the question, "Can you explain the Divinity you claim to experience in Sathya Sai Baba in scientific terms?" Can any one explain the joy caused by an exquisitely beautiful painting in terms of the chemicals which constitute the paints used by the artist? It would make no sense . "A thing of beauty is a joy forever."

It is common knowledge that several thousands of people come to Baba each day seeking His grace and love. This unending stream consists of men and women from all parts of the world, from all religious faiths and from all walks of life. Amongst them are the wealthy and the poor, the young and the aged, the healthy and the sick and so on. They come uninvited, live an austere life in the Ashram and return happy to their homes. Some of them stay on for longer periods and are transformed beyond recognition. Others feel happy with a short stay. Almost every one desires to repeat the experience and does so if he can get a chance. What is the religion that attracts such huge numbers of people from diverse faiths to come and come so often to Him? What is the quality that such people find in Him which they do not find elsewhere? Undoubtedly, the answer is His love, the universal and Divine compassion that He radiates. He has declared so often that there is only one religion and that is the religion of love. He is the embodiment of love. "Love is God. Live in love," so He says and puts it into practice in His own life, each day and every day. People who are hungry for such love and who do not find it anywhere in the world of today where they live and spend their daily lives, flock to Him for this reason, find it in Him in an ample measure, do not want to leave Him if they can help it. They hover round Him like humans who have discovered their lost treasure or like the bees who have discovered a new and rich source of honey. If this is not Divinity, what else is Divinity?

Others, who are not casual visitors but who have the opportunity of experiencing Him a little more closely, easily notice the uncommon and superhuman aspects of His personality. In Bhagavad Gita, the traditionally accepted virtues of prosperity, victory, determination, morality and goodness have been associated with the presence of the Avatar of Krishna, the Yogeswara. Practically everyone who spends a few days in and around the Ashram, where Bhagavan Baba is present, will begin to associate with His presence the four virtues of Sathya (Truth), Dharma (Righteousness), Santhi (Peace) and Prema (Love). A little introspection will show that these are only new names, better suited and more needed in the modern age. In spirit and in essence, the human form and the name we are using today are no different from the human form and the name of Sri Krishna used in the Bhagavad Gita to describe the Avatar of that era. Baba Himself frequently refers to Sathya, Dharma, Santhi and Prema as the four cardinal pillars or the foundation over which the mansion of our eternal Dharma has been built and has to rest for all time for the good of the human race. If this is not the voice of the Creator spoken through Himself incarnated in human form, whose else is God's voice?

In the multi-splendoured and many faceted personality of Bhagavan Baba, one notices an unruffled equanimity and an unchanging and continual awareness and bliss. He is awareness itself, for it does not take many people or much time to discover that He is fully aware of the past, present and future of each individual who is fortunate enough to come to His notice. Moreover, He is aware of what is happening in each and every sphere of human activity, in each and every corner of the created world. In the common worldly sense, His schooling has been next to nothing. Yet, He quotes freely from the scriptures like the Vedas and the Sastras. He astonishes the listeners by quoting from scriptures like the Bible and the Qoran, thus going beyond all limitations of language, time and country. He holds always meaningful and sometimes critically significant conversations with persons who have acquired scholarly proficiency in one area or other such as science, philosophy, law, business and so on. When one is transfixed by such a situation, what is the use of asking a question, "Can you explain this in scientific terms?" It makes no sense. Such and many other similar shattering experiences have led the present speaker to come to the only possible conclusion that while human beings have to acquire knowledge and a limited part at that, by devoting a life-time, Bhagavan Baba is born with the knowledge and is the source of all knowledge - finite and infinite.

Let me now recall the Indian scripture, "Sathyam, Jnanam, Anantham Brahma." Truth, Wisdom and Infinitude constitute

Brahman, the unmanifested God. We have no alternative to exclaiming, if this manifestation in Baba is not Truth, Wisdom and Infinitude, what else is it?

The indefatigable physical energy which He often displays, His defiance of medical norms, His frequently transcending laws of science which scientists regard as being normally inviolable are some examples of the inexplicable actions of Baba. Without spending too much time describing the commonly noticed features of His myriad faceted personality, I will pass on to the deeper and more basic philosophical aspects of a Divine Incarnation or an Avatar. An Incarnation is the word we use in the English language to describe the phenomenon of God appearing in human form. Avatar is the nearest equivalent in Sanskrit, although their root meanings differ to some extent. Divinity, God, Brahman are again words which are all used in English and Sanskrit respectively to convey certain concepts. The interpretation, that the word God stands for the unseen primordial source of power from which creation has emanated in the beginning of time and into which all of it will be dissolved when a catastrophic end comes, is likely to command the widest possible acceptance. Strangely, the Indian concept of Brahman is very much the same. Following is a free translation of what the Upanishads say about Brahman.

"The primordial principle, 'tad ekam,' the uncharacterizable, that which is without any attributes even negative ones, undescribable, unmanifested, the absolute which is beyond being and knowledge, the super-personal in its utter transcendence of all created beings is Brahman." In this context, the Hindu way of looking at creation is to state that, "Nature is the world of objectivization, of alienation, of determinability." The distinctions between man and man, man and woman, dark and fair, fat and slim, are all related to the human body and its form. Despite these differences of form, they all have a common inner non-objective existence. The Eternal Spirit is the same in all, in animals as in men, in learned scholars as in lowly humans. The following Sanskrit verse is of importance.

Asti bhati priyam rupam nama cety amsapanchakam

Adyam trayam brahmarupam jagadrupam tato dwayam

Using the English equivalents and simpler Sanskrit words, the same can be expressed as in the following: Sat (Being), Chit (Awareness), Ananda (Bliss), Rupa (Form), Nama (Name), are the five basic constituents. The first three are of the Brahman, the two that follow are of the world.

Sat, Chit and Ananda perceived in a human form are the Divine aspects of the Eternal in him. They are also called the Swarupa Lakshanas, attributes of the pristine Eternal form. On the other hand, the name and form are temporary attributes (Tatastha Lakshanas) assumed during the life-time of the embodied soul. Against the background of these concepts, it follows that the being, the extraordinary awareness and the continually radiating bliss that we find in Sathya Sai Baba are the Swarupa Lakshanas of the unmanifested God. The name and form of Baba are the Tatastha Lakshanas of the manifested Avatar, the Incarnation of Sathya Sai of the contemporary times. For this reason, the age in which we are living may truly and justifiably be called the "Golden Age."

In His discourses, Baba has often dealt with the roles in our daily lives of spirituality on the one hand and science on the other. The goal of all spiritual quests and the goal of all sciences is to have a vision or an understanding of the nature of the ultimate reality. There can be no serious controversy about such a statement.

To a question, "Can reality have facets that are incompatible with each other?" Arnold Toynbee, an internationally known historian and philosopher, replied:

"Even the fraction of the universe that the human mind can know by applying scientific reasoning to experience matter, at the infinitesimal extremity of its gamut, is now said to have mutually incompatible properties."

Incompatibility that cannot be resolved by human thought is, I think, an indication that we have reached one of the limits of our capacity for understanding. It seems probable that the nature of ultimate reality is only partially comprehensible to human minds."

An alternative way of saying the same thing would be to accept that it is the human comprehension and not the reality that contains the contradictions. Thus, whenever one comes across a conflict between the path of spirituality and the path of science to reach the goal, it makes no sense if the aspirant in each case asserts the inviolability of his own conclusion and refuses to see the other point of view. Science is essentially the result of an age-long sharpening of man's intellect and his sensory functions. The consequent comprehension that man has achieved has its limitations. All thinkers who accept such a limitation have dealt with it by talking of man having become an intellectual giant but having remained a moral dwarf. The same is expressed differently by saying that man's moral immaturity is not compatible with his scientific prowess. Against such a background, spirituality and science do not contradict each other. On the contrary, they complement each other, because their paths are different, their tools are different, but the goals of their quest are the same. A spiritualist seeks to have an understanding of the ultimate reality in visualizing the Creator, the primordial God power behind the created world which is the omnipotent and omnipresent but unmanifested, Divinity, the objective of all spiritual quests. A scientist also seeks to have an understanding of the same ultimate reality, but through a study of the Creator's created world, the only way in which the Creator projects Himself or manifests Himself.

Each one of these two paths has its own successes and failures, its own merits and demerits and above all its own limitations, constraints and regions of validity. The spiritual method deals with the embodied self and the regions which are beyond the realm of bodily perceptions and sensory organs. On the contrary, the scientific method takes man's sensory perceptions as its basic tools. This clear distinction has been repeatedly pointed out by Baba in His discourses by stating that a study of science is needed for living a meaningful daily life in this world, whereas a study of spirituality is needed for making one's daily life not only meaningful but also purposeful from the point of view of the ultimate reality.

In fact, Baba stresses the close connection which exists between spirituality and one's daily life. If one lives one's daily life without fear of sin and without faith in God, reserving both of them for the few moments which one spends in the temple or in the church, practice of virtue will be confined to the four walls of the church. The society will soon come to consist of inhuman human beings. Man will only proclaim that he should love his neighbour as he would love himself when he is in his place of worship, but will begin to hate him in practice during his daily life outside the temple. Brotherhood of man and fatherhood of God will become meaningless platform statements. Love and affection will only be preached but never practised. In fact, Sathya Sai Baba, while powerfully drawing attention to this state of affairs which prevails amongst most communities today, cautions His listeners to become aware of the fact that spirituality and daily life are, indeed, not essentially different. Science has come to be concerned so much with man's daily life in the current era that if his actions are not tempered with a spiritual attitude, the human race is likely to make a mess of itself. It is in this context that Sathya Sai Baba's views and expositions of spirituality and of science have a contemporary significance. Indeed, they have a survival value to the human race as a whole.

At this point, I will record a few statements, which we frequently come across in the scriptures of India and which are often repeated by Sathya Sai Baba in His discourses. The Creator and His creation are not different from each other. Service to man is service to God. Purusha (Creator) and Prakriti (creation) are like an object and its image. There can be no image, if there is no object. There can be no creation if there is no creator. God and Nature are, therefore, inextricably connected with each other, as the reverse and the obverse of a coin. Spiritual aspects of a man's life cannot be separated from his daily routine related to his living in this world as one member of the community. The entire creation can be regarded as a projection of the creator. In summary, one can proceed to have a vision of the creator only through His creation. Science is a study - with certain constraints - of the created world and the laws that govern the same. How can there be any conflict between a spiritual quest for knowing the Creator and a scientist's endeavour to reach the Creator through a systematic study of the Creator's creation?

The foregoing is a brief summary of Sathya Sai Baba's pronouncements regarding spirituality and science. In fact, realizing that presence of Vignana (logical knowledge) and absence of Pragnana (intuitive wisdom) have been the main features of man's learning process in the past few centuries, Baba has initiated the scheme of Pragnana Pradarshan by way of museums depicting science-cum-spiritual achievements of man. This has been a laudable attempt at educating the youth in spiritual matters in a non-formal way.

It is with great pleasure I have reproduced Dr. Bhagavantam's discourse, hoping that the reader will find it as interesting and rewarding as I do.

The Model for Love
Sathya Sai Baba

A brilliant model of unselfish service for us all is the Avatar Bhagavan Sri Sathya Sai Baba. Already in His early childhood He gave proof of His love for His fellowmen by His unselfish service. During His entire life He has indefatigably served human beings with divine love. Everything He does, He does for us.

Sai Baba says, "Out of free will I have taken this human body for re-establishing Dharma - righteousness - among all humanity. I shall not rest until My mission is finished. My life is My message."

All people live in Sai Baba's ashram under the same simple conditions with one prayer, one wish, to at least once have an interview with Him. Sai Baba knows everything about us and, in the first instance, calls for an interview those who most are in need of His help.

Many have undertaken great trials and sacrifices in coming to Sai Baba. One day, for instance, I saw a great lorry parked within the ashram area. It had arrived from Northern India. A platform formed two floors, and was covered by a big tarpaulin. On this uncomfortable lorry about thirty persons had travelled, women and children in the lower section and men in the upper part. It had taken them seven days to come to Puttaparthi, to Sai Baba - a long, arduous journey. They cooked meals, ate and slept on the two levels. It is not easy for a Westerner to imagine how this could be possible, but for these devotees it was. They stayed two days with Sai Baba before they returned home under the burning sun of India and often along very bad roads.

I talked with one of the men and expressed my admiration that they with women and children had managed to tolerate such a long and trying trip. With folded palms the man turned towards the temple, beaming with happiness, and said, "I'm very happy. We are all very happy for having received Sai Baba's darshan. No hardships are too difficult to overcome through the grace of our Lord Sai Baba."

This was indeed an inspiring, joyful experience to see and hear this man talk. I felt pretty small and pitiable when I stood before him and thought of how I had grumbled and complained about mosquitoes disturbing my sleep and other similar trivialities in my comfortable flat. It was an elevating and instructive experience to witness such devotion as this brave group exemplified.

The man gave me his visiting card and said that I was welcome to visit him if I went to Northern India. I felt great respect and reverence for both him and all the others in the group. We bowed and took farewell with mutual respect.

Belief and love can move mountains, and one who also has a contented heart is indeed a happy man. I had the feeling that the man I had talked to was a happy man. He radiated light, love and humility.

Sai Baba's social work and its development over the years inspires me with great admiration. One asks indeed how it has been possible to bring about so much in such a short time. To build up schools, hospitals and extensive service activities in various fields of social life, working well all over the country, is indeed a divine achievement.

I regret not having exact and up-to-date information at hand, but as far as I know there are now a number of colleges, which have been developed to a very high degree. The college at Puttaparthi has been deemed a university and is known as the Sri Sathya Sai Institute For Higher Learning. It is reported to be the only university to receive full accreditation under the Indian system since Independence. Recently a modern Planetarium was constructed here.

It is hardly necessary to mention that in all Sai educational institutions, besides the usual subjects of study, the greatest importance is laid on moral and spiritual education. It is Sai

Baba's intention that His pupils shall have such an education that when they later begin to serve their country and fellow men, they shall carry out their duties standing on a firm moral ground.

All over the world we experience problems and conflicts, which are difficult to solve on account of lack of moral attitudes. Within all fields of society one finds mostly selfish motives behind the solution of problems. So it is also in the highest ranks of political parties which are chosen to govern the country. How can one then expect that people in the community shall feel social responsibility? Hypocrisy is all too common. The most egoistic motives are often hidden behind a pious mask.

It is necessary that we change our attitudes as soon as possible, and in a more selfless way take responsibility for our actions as members of society. Only then we can change our society in a positive direction.

Sai Baba is aware of today's social problems and sees clearly man's moral decay, which is going on at all levels of society. In His early youth, Sai Baba started the great and difficult work to teach us to realize that the condition for achieving a positive change in our development is that the ground for this transformation is laid already in the earliest years. A school cannot do much without well-educated teachers, who themselves are good models for their pupils both within and outside the school. Also parents must understand and take their share of the responsibility. The quality of nurturing in the home is for the child of greatest importance.

Education in Human Values, (E.H.V.), is a subject that Sai Baba founded several years ago for schools at all levels of education. A great number of teachers receive training in this subject in Puttaparthi or Whitefield, where Sai Baba arranges training courses from time to time. The Indian Government has already to a great extent included this important approach in the curricula of all schools. In several other countries the development is going in the same direction, along the lines drawn up by Sai Baba.

We must learn to live in accordance with the divine message of love. Serve and love your neighbour irrespective of race and religion. Then we are serving and loving God. Not until then do we show that we have correctly understood Sathya Sai Baba's divine message of love.

Sai Baba's Omnipresence

During one of our visits to Sai Baba we stayed a few days in the Hotel Shilton in Bangalore. When we visited Brindavan for darshan one morning He called us for an interview.

He first addressed me with the words, "In your home in Stockholm you called for Me so it could be heard in the whole cosmos." The reason for this had been that I had fallen headlong about two metres. My back was seriously injured when striking a massive iron bar that stuck out from a gymnastics stand. On this occasion I was alone and lost consciousness for a while because of the tremendous pain. I couldn't move and thought I had broken my spine. As soon as I was able, I grasped the locket that Sai Baba had given me, and which was hanging around my neck. I shouted with the full strength of my lungs, "Sai Baba, help me! Help me, Sai Baba!" Next moment I felt a wave of heat rise over my back, and the pain was mitigated. After a while I could get up. When I later inspected my back I found it had been severely damaged, with a gash in the lumbar region. After only a few days I was miraculously healed.

"Yes, Sai Baba! I shouted indeed so that it could be heard in the entire cosmos! Thank You for hearing me and coming to my rescue!"

Similar experiences have occurred to many of Sai Baba's devotees all over the world. In a critical situation or times of great distress remembrance of Sai Baba has brought about a relief of the situation. Some devotees have been fortunate to receive a materialised ring, bracelet or other gift from Sai Baba. When wearing these objects they are reminded of His omnipresence. Sai Baba says that if we are in a difficult situation, keep the object He has given us in our hand and call for Him. He will hear our call and come to our rescue. Of course Sai Baba's grace is such that we can receive help even if it does not occur to us to think of Him just at that critical moment.

When Sai Baba gave me the locket He said, "This locket will always protect you. I'm always with you." Quite instinctively I had grasped it in my hand and called for Sai Baba's help. He heard my call, intervened and helped me at that very moment. Later I heard of or read about many similar occurences. Sai Baba is always present. In His love and grace He protects and helps His devotees who call for Him, wherever in the world they may be. May we always receive Sai Baba's divine gifts of love and grace with faith and confidence.

Sai Baba expressed His happiness to see us again. Then He moved His hand in a circular motion several times and materialized for me a gold ring with His portrait. We parted again with the same words as the day before, "We see each other tomorrow."

In the evening I felt feverish and had a sore throat. The night was sleepless and by the morning I had developed a full cold. I found it best to stay in my room to recuperate. Sisko would go to Brindavan. I asked her, if possible, to convey to Sai Baba my regrets that I could not come, as I was not feeling well. I waved Sisko off when she left by taxi together with another lady, who was severely handicapped and glad of a helping hand.

When left alone I turned on the tape recorder, listened to bhajans and thought of Sai Baba. I prayed, sat thereafter for meditation and experienced a wonderful quiet peace inside. How long a time I had been sitting in this state I do not know, but when I opened my eyes Sai Baba stood smiling before me in the room, surrounded by a brilliant light. It was difficult to believe my eyes. Did I dream this? Was I in a state of hallucination or what? Thoughts flew through my head - and Sai Baba was still standing there with the same smile on His face!

I was unable to say a single word. As suddenly as Sai Baba had come, He disappeared. I shook my head and had some water. I didn't understand anything of what I had just experienced.

Hours passed by, and Sisko returned from Brindavan. Beaming with happiness she told me that Sai Baba had come up to her and asked for me. She informed Him that I had caught a cold and therefore stayed in the hotel room to recover. When Sai Baba heard this He had stood a while silent before her and then said, "Bring him tomorrow here to me."

After Sai Baba had left me in the hotel room I felt much better. I told Sisko about my experience, and she was as astonished as I - we did not understand it. What I had experienced we had not previously heard about. Miracles like this were entirely strange to us, but we felt, of course, very happy.

The next day I felt fully recovered and accompanied Sisko to Brindavan. Sai Baba came out, gave His darshan and invited us to come in. He led us into a room where we were alone, smiled at me and asked how I felt. I couldn't but thank Him for my again being healthy and asked, "Please, Sai Baba, do explain what it was that happened yesterday morning in my hotel room in Bangalore. Did I have a hallucination, or what was it?" "No, as you couldn't come to me, I came to you. I'm always with you. And then your illness was gone."

It took a long time for me to understand that it really was true, that which I had experienced. It was reality that Sai Baba had appeared to me in my hotel room at the same time as He had been entirely visible and real for His devotees during darshan in Brindavan. Later on both Sisko and I heard and read that Sai Baba is able to appear to His devotees, in His physical body, at several places at the same time. Many have witnessed and will witness similar bilocation phenomena. Sai Baba has, for instance, been actively working in Puttaparthi and at the same time appeared in Bombay to several of His devotees. He has, on the spot, materialized and given them pieces of jewellery. One can read about similar events in literature about Sai Baba.

I felt deeply grateful and richly blessed by the divine visit in my hotel room in Bangalore.

Later I came to understand that it is not unusual for holy and enlightened beings to possess this power to appear at several places at the same time, fully visible for those who have asked for help in a difficult situation. In the Vedic scriptures it is described how Gods in similar ways and on various occasions have appeared to their devotees, at the same time as their physical body has been at other places far away.

Jesus let His disciples experience a similar miracle, when He came to meet them on the Lake of Gennesaret whilst they were out fishing. They had been startled by a violent storm, which threatened to overturn their boat and they were frightened to death. Then Jesus came surrounded by light, walking on the waves, calmed the storm and rescued His disciples from being drowned.

The Italian holy Capuchin friar Padre Pio, who died in 1968 at the age of eighty one years, at the tender age of five years had an impulse to offer his life to God. He was one of those figures, like Jesus, whom God now and then sends to Earth and who know it to be their duty to lead souls to God. Padre Pio was, without doubt, one of the most prominent, spiritually developed beings of our time in the West. God had given him many spiritual gifts, among them the power of bilocation. Descriptions of his life confirm several events when Padre Pio has appeared at the same time at different places to help people, who in their distress have called on him for help.

These are only a few examples how God's power manifests itself and works through the holy, to whom God has given the power to comprehend and answer people's call for help. This possibility to make contact is not limited to only the bodily existence. There are many evidences of how these holy ones, even after their death, have appeared in answer to people's prayers. God appears to us in the form which we hold most dearly, that is, in which we choose to worship Him. Sai Baba's appearance simultaneous at several places is for Him as easy as it is for us to turn a page in the book we read.

I cannot give any scientific explanation for this phenomenon and miracles Sai Baba performs, which to us seem incomprehensible. But thousands have been present and can bear witness to this reality. Sai Baba says, "It lies outside your limited capacity to understand My divine unlimited nature." And what is science? It represents only the level of knowledge one is on today, the sum of past experiences. One single new discovery can overthrow all that one earlier has built up!

In the mandir in Prasanthi Nilayam I was reminded about a vision I had in my youth in Sweden. I stood in a square in a town in a foreign country. People's dress and the entire surroundings were strange to me. My eyes were drawn to an older man who stood at some distance. He had a white beard and he radiated light and love. He lifted his hand and made a sign to me to come closer. I approached him and looked into a pair of mild, loving eyes. When our eyes met I felt a stream of warmth within and my heart was filled with love for him. Without words I understood what he meant, "I'm waiting for you." The vision dissolved and I was again sitting in my room in Sweden.

When I now, over 30 years later, saw a.portrait of Shirdi Baba in the mandir in Puttaparthi, I thought I recognized the man I had met in the vision. During all those years I had often thought of this vision, but had not understood its significance. But now I felt intuitively that I had earlier lived close to Sai Baba in His incarnation as Shirdi Baba. It was this Sai Baba had meant when He said to me, "You have lived very close to Me in an earlier life." The happiness at meeting again filled my heart.

Sai Baba scatters His love and grace over His devotees in selfless service twenty-four hours a day, far beyond human capacity. He is never separated from His devotees, wherever in the world they may be. Our body is God's temple, and in our heart He is constantly with us. God does not know about any separation; for Him no dualism exists; in God we are one and the same. Sai Baba says, "I am the invisible atman, the sovereign absolute. God is in man, man is in God. What seems to be many is in reality one."

Sai Baba's Miracles

How do Sai Baba's miracles come about? Sai Baba has Himself explained at an unique interview He gave to Sri R.K. Karanjia, the chief editor of the Bombay journal "Blitz," in 1976.

Question: What meaning has the Vibhuti and the ornaments that You materialize and give people? Is there any need for a God-man to demonstrate miracles which any magician can perform?

Baba: In My case, this is an evidence of My divinity. It is by no means a show of divine capacity. Magic performances are given, as you know, for earning money. It is a question of tricks that the magician carries out. It is a kind of legalized cheating, transferring an object from one place to another by means of trickery and sleight of hand. They do not possess any siddhis or occult powers.

What I do is an act of quite another kind, an act of creation. It is neither magic, nor siddhi powers. Firstly, I do not want to have anything in return. Secondly, I do not transfer things, I create them. I don't do this out of any kind of need or wish to show My powers. For Me this is a kind of "visiting card" for convincing people of My love for them and to secure their devotion in return. Since love is formless, I do materializations as proof of My love. They are only symbols.

Question: Anyhow, I do not understand why You materialize rings, watches, lockets and similar showy ornaments?

Baba: Most people want to have a talisman that symbolizes My protection, so I give it to them. When they are in distress they feel the grasp of the ring, the watch or the bracelet and remember Me. They call for Me so that I can assist them. On the other hand, if I give them something they cannot wear, they put it aside and forget it. The main thing is that those ornaments or talismans, whatever you prefer to call them, give people the feeling of safety and protection they need during crises and difficulties. They create a symbolic link over the great distance between Me and them. When the devotee needs Me, these objects mediate the message at lightning speed and I come at once to help them.

Question: I'm sorry for being stubborn, but does one not cheat the company or break its patent if one gives for instance an Omega-watch?

Baba: I can assure you, it is not at all a question of something like that. It would be to cheat the company or break a patent if it were a question of transferring a watch from one place to another. But I do not transfer, I entirely create. Whatever I want, I materialize instantaneously. I do not know of any company that has complained of any breach of a patent.

Question: How about the Vibhuti You materialize? We would like to know how it is done, as Your critics try to discredit You by sending around magicians who make similar kind of Vibhuti.

Baba: What I materialize is a divine creation with a powerful significance and symbolism. It is a symbol for the cosmic, immortal and boundless nature of God, the Atman or the Spirit, or in other words that which is left when everything worldly, temporary and transmutable has been burnt away. I have told you about the importance of a life without desires. After Shiva had burnt to a heap of ash the God of desires, Kama, He adorned Himself with the ash to show that He was the conqueror of desires. When Kama was conquered, Prema reigned as the Goddess of Love. That is the meaning and significance of the ash. "From earth you have come, earth you shall become." Ash or earth is the final state of objects. It cannot go through any more alterations. In a spiritual connection it constitutes a warning for the recipient to give up, to burn up all passions, bonds and temptations, to become pure in thought, word and deed. It is for impressing this lesson on men's minds that I materialize ash for those who come to Me with love and devotion. Like the other materializations it constitutes a talisman that heals the sick and gives protection for the needy. It is a symbol for the divine, entirely different from the magicians' tricks, which you mentioned.

Question: It is said that You have carried out miracles, even revived the dead or saved people from accidents at a long distance. You have carried out at distant places, controlled surgical operations which were examined by medical experts. How do You manage to do things like that?

Baba: Through My own sankalpa, that is, divine will and power. As an Avatar this power is inherent, inborn, total and natural for My will. I do not need any mantra, no sadhana, no tantra and no yantra for performing these so-called miracles; they are natural for My state. My powers are simply the expression of the divine reality which merges Me with everything, everywhere, during all times and at all places. Miracles belong to the expression of the boundless power of God. Coming to the main point of your question, healing has two aspects. I can cure, rescue and also revive people, if they are in a spiritually receptive state. It is like the positive and the negative currents in electricity. My capacity to heal can be compared with the positive current. Your devotion for Me is the negative current. When these two are united, devotion contributes to what is called miraculous healing.

It is in fact the mind of man which is responsible for both the sickness and the cure. He himself is the cause or origin. Consequently, concerning healing, the necessary faith for the purpose must exist in his mind. All I do is to give him confidence, the will and the power to cure himself. It is My abundant love in interaction with the intensity of the devotee's faith in Me, which brings about the result aimed at.

Question: So it is not a question of siddhi powers or magic tricks, as Your critics venture to allege?

Baba: It is neither a question of magic tricks nor siddhi powers. These anybody can get through discipline and the right yoga-exercises, but My powers to protect, heal and save people and materialize, arise in God and can only be used by an Avatar. They are in no way planned for, trained or developed, but flow out from the cosmic force.

Question: Some people declare that You command invisible spirits who can move objects from one place to another by Your order.

Baba: There is no need for Me to command invisible spirits, as My own divine will materializes the objects. I am everything, everywhere, omnipotent and omnipresent. Whatever I will, happens instantaneously. Like the qualities truth, love and peace, these phenomena are of the kind that have an effect on the atmic or cosmic powers behind the universe.

Question: Devotees both here at home and abroad claim that they have positive evidence of Your presence in their hearts. Some have written about You as their inherent God. What is the explanation for this phenomenon?

Baba: That is the grace brought forth out of My love for them in interaction with their devotion. We all belong to the same divine principle. The divine which is in all as a small spark, is in Me as the full flame, and it is My mission to develop each little spark of God to the full divine flame. The basis for this development is that he who gets grace also on his part has the necessary devotion. Those who carry Baba's presence as an inherent God in their heart belong to this kind of devotee. They come to Me, see and hear Me, experience My love for them and reciprocate it with devotion. Thus they become part of Me and My divinity.

Thus far the interview.

Dr. Erlendur Haraldsson, parapsychologist at the University of Iceland in Reykjavik, has written a very interesting and readable book, "Miracles are My Visiting Cards," about Sai Baba. Together with Dr. Karlis Osis from the American Society for Psychical Research in New York he made several research journeys to India for studying at close quarters the inexplicable phenomena which have taken place near Sai Baba.

Through their own observations and interviews with many people, they have found out that those who have testified to Sai Baba's miracles have experienced them in reality. Sai Baba is omniscient. He creates and dematerializes various objects. Dr. Haraldsson and Dr. Osis have also gathered considerable evidence that Vibhuti (sacred ash) as well as Amrit (nectar) have appeared on portraits of Sai Baba in homes of devotees all over the world. Many have also experienced how Sai Baba has appeared physically when they called for help because of an accident or severe illness, something I can also certify. Sai Baba's capacity to appear at the same time at various places has been experienced by many. Even in dreams of devotees Sai Baba can come to give advice or for curing sickness. He can also be visible for His devotees or doubters in the guise of different Gods to prove His identity with previous Avatars.

Also of great interest is the following statement by the well-known parapsychologist and aura-scientist Frank G. Barnowski, who in Arizona is carrying out research work concerning the human aura. He states, after having personally studied Sai Baba's aura, "I had heard so much about Sathya Sai Baba, from many of my intellectual colleagues, university rectors, physicists, psychiatrists, people who had contacted Him and who since then were completely changed. I had heard so much about what He can do, His capacity to heal, to contact people in a telepathic way, to help them.

Early one Sunday morning I saw Him standing on the balcony (of His residence in Brindavan) and blessing the many devotees who stood and sang below. The aura around Sai Baba was beyond everything that one could imagine. It was entirely unbelievable. The white was five to seven times the size around an ordinary human being. This shows the energy. But behind this pattern there was the blue, which was limitless. Behind this there were gold and silver bands. The aura that emanated from Swami was different from all the auras of human individuals I have ever seen. The fact is, that it radiated wide around the limited building He was standing at."

"I observed Sai Baba during more than a week when He moved among people morning and evening. I observed His aura, which mostly had blue bands when He moved amidst people, which signifies spirituality, and pale-red bands which were beyond every notion. Pale-red means for a scientist boundless unselfish love."

"Sometimes Baba went up to people and touched them. It was amazing to see how negativism in their auras suddenly was activated with positive feelings, and when He went on, it was like part of His aura or energy had melted together with their auras. His energy seems to be inexhaustible, He never gets tired."

"I observed Him when He went up to a small girl sitting in a wheelchair and fondled with her. I was amazed at the loving aura that surrounded Him. It seems like His aura definitely shows His love for people. I have met several of these holy men, but none of them has made himself so easy to approach and affable for their people as He has made."

"I risk my reputation in making this statement, but two days ago I saw into Sai Baba's eyes; they have a glow I haven't seen in anybody else."

"It was quite evident for me that I looked into the face of Divinity. As per my opinion, Sai Baba is exactly what He pretends to be, what He wants you to be and what He represents - Love. And that is exactly what He is . . .nothing but love."

Sai Baba and His Devotees

Sai Baba says, "All names are Mine and all forms are Mine. There is no need for you to change the God you have chosen to worship and choose another after you have seen and heard me." People belonging to different religions are all equally welcome to Sai Baba. Truth is higher than religion.

Bhakti, love for God, means to direct one's feelings and thoughts towards God. It is the road that leads to devotion and merger in God.

At a personal meeting with Sai Baba the experience of divine grace and love is overwhelming and remains in the heart of the devotee. Sai Baba materializes and makes gifts to His devotees as an encouragement and proof of the loving relationship that exists between them.

To love and be devoted to God implies to love God in all living beings, including one's own divine self. When desires, anger and hatred have been replaced by love, we experience divine peace. Our efforts to understand and become conscious of God's reality blossom of their own accord. A devotee's yearning to selflessly serve God with love evokes God's grace. Sai Baba says, "If you take one step towards Me, I shall take ten steps towards you."

In India and the rest of the world there are approximately thirty-five to forty million Sai devotees, and the number continues to grow like a rolling snowball. Sai Baba's devotees see Him as an Avatar, a Divine Incarnation. He says, "I have incarnated and taken this mortal body of My own free will to lead mankind back to its origin, God."

An Avatar is God embodied in human form, and is born with a divine pure consciousness. To stand before Sai Baba and experience His divine radiation is a great privilege and divine grace. His power of inspiration follows us and helps us in our spiritual endeavours towards fulfilment in God. Sai Baba says, "Everyone of you is an Avatar. You are like Me, the divine wrapped in flesh and bone. The difference is that I always have been aware of it, whereas you are not conscious of this truth. The reality is that I am you and you are I. There is no difference. What seems so is nothing but an illusion. You are the waves, I am the ocean. Experience this and be free, be divine." Sai Baba speaks out of His higher divine consciousness and knows that He is divine. The ordinary man is still at such a low level of consciousness that he cannot understand that he is also divine. The truth is that our immortal soul and higher consciousness is God. Therefore we ought to meditate on God in our heart and become conscious of our inherent divinity.

In India a spiritual teacher is called "guru." Sai Baba is, of course, His devotees' guru. He is addressed by His name or "Swami," (Master). Many have never had a spiritual teacher, but have nevertheless reached the goal of liberation. Our life experiences which lead us spiritually forward are also our guru. Our intellect and spiritual exercises are the means we use to know our divine inner self, the true "I." Within ourselves there is the highest of all gurus, God, always present. If we learn to listen to the divine Presence in our heart, we have a continuous and infallible contact with our true guru.

If we serve God with sincere love, He will purify our heart and lift our consciousness into the light of the soul. We carry within a spark of God's flame. If we take care of this spark well, foster it with love and selfless thoughts and deeds, it will develop into a burning fire in our inner being.

The spiritual development of a person leads him or her, life after life, from a lower to a higher level of consciousness, to finally merge in the pure divine consciousness, becoming one with God. This is the true meaning of our life and the goal for our spiritual development here on Earth.

We ourselves create our good fortune as well as our misfortune. Our selfish ego is responsible for the set-backs Our thoughts and deeds decide our fate. Therefore it is important that we learn to discipline our mind and bring our thoughts under conscious control. Discipline, spiritual practices, protect us against the influence of the ego. A humble heart helps us to live in love. We must fight against our ego which keeps us bound to the illusory, transitory world of materialism. We must let the light of the soul give us power and wisdom to liberate ourselves from ignorance. God is reality. God is life. God is love. Love liberates us from the bonds of the ego. Love makes us free. Love gives us peace in our heart.

This way to God, to immortality, is what Sai Baba has come to teach us. His life is His message. He lives for His devotees and works without rest for our spiritual development. Sai Baba calls His so-called miracles His "visiting cards." They are but natural means in God's hands for enticing us seemingly ignorant ones to Him, to listen to Him and learn of Him. He with His divine radiation, with the power of love, can then transform us and lead us home to our origin, God.

Avatars

The Indian epic, the Mahabharata, comprises about one hundred thousand verses. The Gods, Brahma, Vishnu and Shiva, are depicted as the principle Deities. They are three different aspects of the cosmic life energy, Brahman. Brahma creates the world, Vishnu maintains it and Shiva dissolves it. Their qualities are the three so-called gunas. One interpretation is Rajas is the active, the creating, Sattwas is the pure, the maintaining, and Thamas is the dissolving, the dull. These three gunas are also represented in man and stand for the eternal renewal and transformation process that is continuous in all creation.

In the Mahabharata it is told how Brahma requested and persuaded Vishnu to be born on Earth to save the world, which was oppressed by demons and was threatened with ruin.

The word "Avatar" means revelation, incarnatation or descent. The first Avatar who incarnated on Earth in human form was the God Vishnu. He had at His disposal all God's creative power. He governed all creation in the entire universe, microcosm and macrocosm, and was omnipresent.

Later Vishnu again incarnated on Earth and took human form as the Avatar Rama, to save the world from the grasp of the demon king, Ravana. In the Indian epic Ramayana, it is told how Rama and the "monkey God," Hanuman, released the Goddess Sita, who had been kept in captivity by Ravana on the island Lanka (Sri Lanka, previously Ceylon).

The reincarnation of Vishnu as the Avatar Krishna is a further divine form of revelation, just as Rama had been. One of the main missions of Krishna was to initiate Arjuna into the divine truths that are recorded in the Bhagavad Gita, the Song of God, for the benefit of all humanity. The Avatar Krishna reveals to Arjuna His divine nature saying, "Though I am the unborn, of eternal nature, and though I am the all powerful Lord of all worlds, I nevertheless take physical form by My own power, in perfect fullness, when Dharma, (righteousness), falls and Adharma, (unrighteousness), arises. Then, oh Arjuna, I send Myself out." Krishna says further to Arjuna, "Seek shelter and refuge in Me alone, and I shall lead you to the goal."

A Poorna-Avatar (full Avatar) is the highest divine revelation in human form. Very few have had the good fortune to recognize the God-Avatar. Not even Arjuna, who was a great hero and highly evolved being in his time, knew Krishna's divine reality. Not until he was ready and asked for it did Krishna show Himself in all His divine perfection and splendour.

An Avatar incarnates of His own free will, chooses His parents, His body and the place and time for His earthly birth. He is already from the beginning conscious of His divinity. He is always in the highest state of consciousness, almighty, omniscient, omnipresent. He knows the past, the present and the future. He is always full of bliss and love. An Avatar is not limited to His body. He is everywhere and in everything. He has full control of the elements of nature; He can make rain fall or cease at will. What He wishes, that He creates. He is one with all in the cosmic creation. He knows the thoughts of His devotees, their wishes, their pains.

On several occasions Sai Baba has taken over the diseases of His devotees and has also revived the dead. When Sai Baba has intervened to save a helpless devotee, who without His intervention would not have survived, there has always been a deeper reason for Him to perform such miraculous healings.

The career of an Avatar is predestined, says Sai Baba. Rama came to re-establish Sathya and Dharma, truth and righteousness. Krishna came to foster Santhi and Prema, peace and love. All these are again in danger, therefore the present Avatar has come.

Sai Baba has declared to His devotees that just as He, Sai Baba, is a reincarnation of Shirdi Baba, He will reincarnate as Prema Baba some years after His bodily departure.

The Avatar Sathya Sai Baba has said on several occasions that there is no human being on this Earth who can fully understand His divine nature, not even by means of science. How can we recognize an Avatar, as long as we are ignorant of our own inner divine being? Our way to Avatarhood is that our consciousness, through numerous earthly sojourns, must develop to a divine level. This way is often both long and laborious. The Avatar, on the other hand, is born with a pure divine cosmic consciousness and in possession of all spiritual powers. He may have a particular mission He has chosen to fulfil. Part of this mission is to guide humanity back to its source, God, the ultimate goal of life.

The Avatar of our age Sri Sathya Sai Baba is identical with Vishnu, who took the earlier form of the Avatars, Rama and Krishna. It is only the outer human form and the time of their incarnation on Earth that is different. In reality they are one. They are divine embodiments of the cosmic life energy, Brahman.

God is Reality

There are a number of world religions. Many battles have been fought over which is the right one. The Avatar Sri Sathya Sai Baba says, "There is only one God. There is only one religion, the religion of love. There is only one race, humanity."

According to Vedic scriptures, when God incarnates in human form He is called an Avatar. The Avatar Krishna reincarnated sixty-three years ago in the small village of Puttaparthi in South India and took human shape as the Avatar Sri Sathya Sai Baba. A divine manifestation in human form is a physical manifestation of the absolute infinite. The creator of the universe Brahman and the Avatar Sathya Sai Baba are identical in their essential divine nature, they are one. Brahman is the ultimate cause for the incarnation of the Indian Avatars Rama, Krishna and Sai Baba. Brahman is the same, as real in the Avatar, in man, in the wind in the top of a tree and in the scent of a flower. An Avatar is born in possession of all spiritual powers and incarnates when Dharma, righteousness, is in great decline, in danger of being overcome by evil. The Avatar thus leads mankind on the correct path and prevents annihilation.

What the Bible is for the Christians and Koran for the Muslims, the Vedic scriptures are for the Hindus. In these scriptures the concept God means spirit, power and energy. Together they constitute the fundamental concept for the primeval force which in the Vedas is called Brahman.

Brahman is the supreme, absolute, eternal, universal creating power behind all cosmic forms and phenomena, which we understand and experience as divine creation. The power of Brahman expresses itself in innumerable forms of creation, known as well as unknown. When we consider what this universal creating power is, we understand that God is immortal spirit and energy, without beginning and without end. The primeval energy we call Brahman is sovereign, uninfluenced, independent, omnipresent and omnipotent. For Hindus these are familiar concepts, but maybe not so for a Westerner who ponders about the reality of God.

One who is anxiously searching for the Truth behind the secrets of the universe asks, "How shall I become conscious of and understand that which I so whole-heartedly want to learn to know, God, the Truth?" One who is familiar with and follows the directions of the Vedas, practises yoga, meditation, to discover God in his or her inner consciousness.

Yoga means union. Practising of yoga teaches us to still our thoughts and purify our consciousness. When we, through meditation, reach the spring of stillness, then we have come into a superconscious, transcendental state of pure divine consciousness and can experience how our real being, our soul, merges in the cosmic soul Brahman. They always were one and always will be one.

Our ego has created an illusory I-consciousness that deceives us and makes us believe that our inner being is separated from the divine soul Brahman, though these in reality are one forever. Not even death can separate us from Brahman. Our body dies and disintegrates to the basic elements, but our soul is eternal.

One who has practised yoga for a long time can experience how the higher Self liberates itself from the lower self. Man is in God and God is in man. The Presence of God is a concrete fact in all creation. In our heart we experience it as love. It has no distinct form. We can neither see it nor touch it, but we feel and experience love as a reality in our life. God is love.

One who has reached lasting success in his or her practice of yoga can experience God's pure consciousness. This state is called Nirvana and means liberation from the lower self. Nirvana is merger with God in a cosmic existence. He or she, who through their own struggle and divine grace has reached these spiritual heights, is rewarded with bliss and peace. This experience cannot be described in words, it is not of this world.

If we only were aware of God's omnipresent spirit, we could also accept oneness of life in everything and live in love with each other, free from religious conflicts. Ramakrishna Paramahamsa once said to his disciples, "God is like a big container filled with water. Out of this container the Hindus, the Muslims and the Christians fetch their water, but they call it by different names. In any case, it is the same water they drink."

Why make war and fight about names, forms and rituals, or which religious community we belong to, when we all worship the only one true God? In the Bhagavad Gita Lord Krishna says, "Whatever outer form you worship, you worship Me, and I shall lead you to the goal." We are all at different stages of development and must not let theological dogmas hide the way and the Truth. Each one believes in his way, and each honest struggle to find God deserves to be treated with respect.

The Avatar Sathya Sai Baba says, "I know that I am God, but you do not know that you also are God." As long as we are not aware of our inner reality, we cannot understand the significance of Sai Baba's words. Two thousand years ago Jesus gave the same message when he said, "Truly I tell you, you are all Gods." We search for God outside ourselves in temples and holy places, on the heights of mountains, but if we instead directed our vision from the outer world to the inner being, we would find God within ourselves, in our heart.

Jesus said, "I am in My Father, the Father is in Me. You are in Me, I am in you. He who has seen Me, has seen the Father." What Jesus meant was all life is one. We are one with the inner being of nature in the entire universal creation. We are a flame of God's reality, which is the ultimate cause for man's existence. We belong to God, we are His creation. Our life is dependent on God, but God is not dependent on us. God expresses Himself through His creating life energy in our body. We can by our own efforts do nothing. We are an image of God, an instrument in His hands.

Our ego has created an illusion that makes us identify ourselves with our body. This illusion makes us believe that it is we who, by our own efforts, are effective within various fields of our activities. We cannot distinguish between illusion and reality. Some can understand more of the secrets of the universe than others. Therefore truth and reality become relative conceptions. All knowledge stands in a certain relationship to something else.

We human beings cannot comprehend God's total reality. Sai Baba says, "How shall the limited be able to understand the limitless!" In a transcendental state we can experience the divine Presence, hear the divine voice in our inner being and obtain answers to the questions of life. Sai Baba's and Jesus' words, "You are all Gods," remain unreal and incomprehensible for us as long as we are not conscious of our own inner divinity. Nor can we comprehend God's true being in other living creatures.

Nothing exists without or can be separated from God's omnipresent spirit. The philosopher Boehme expressed the same when saying, "God is in all and all rests in God." What separates us from Sai Baba and Jesus is that we are not conscious of our inner divinity.

Sai Baba says that we must ask, "Who am I? From where do I come?" and, "Where am I going to?" The school of life implies making us aware of who we really are and understanding that we come from God. We are Gods, and one day we shall return to God. God is life

In deep reverence and humility I bow down to Sai Baba's divine Lotus Feet in gratitude, for He has led me and let me experience God's reality in life. Sai Ram.!

The Eternal Life

Our soul is a ray of the eternal soul, in spirit we are one. This reality confirms that we are born Gods and immortal souls. We are part of the eternal, the limitless, that reveals itself in all the various forms of life. We have always been and will always remain divine. Our true Self is our divine Self in our heart. In Vedic scriptures this is referred to as the "real I."

Our bodies fade and die, but our soul is eternal. It takes on new forms of life, new bodies, in the same way as nature transforms and renews itself. We cannot see our soul or God's creating energy directly, and therefore many deny God's existence. The universal soul is the life energy that maintains life in our body and manifests itself in all creation. It is the same in all forms of life. In this connection I wish to narrate a true story.

An old holy man was approaching a village. He was met by some youngsters who made fun of him, as he asserted that he could see God. One cannot see God, they said. The old man promised to try to explain this matter for the youngsters. However as he was exhausted after a long walk he asked first for a bowl of milk to drink. The youngsters were helpful and quickly fetched some fresh milk. The old man received the bowl with gratitude. He then started intensively and with full concentration to stare at the milk. He stared and stared in silence, and the youngsters began to become impatient. Would he not drink the milk? "Yes," the old man said, "but it is said that there is butter in milk. However intensively I search, I cannot see the least butter here." The youngsters laughed at the old man, it was not possible to see the butter in the milk as simply as that! First one has to treat the milk in particular ways, before one can see the butter. "Oh!" the old man said. "That makes it much easier for me to make you understand that God can be seen! To see God the mind of man, exactly like the milk, has to be treated in a special way, using meditative spiritual exercises. Not until that has been done, can one see God. It is exactly the same as with butter, particular actions are needed to obtain the desired result."

To deny God's existence is ignorance. Electricity is also invisible, formless energy, but it makes the lamp in our room give light, and we use this power in numerous ways in our daily life. Just as electricity gives light to the lamp, so the divine energy expresses itself through our body. We are instruments for God, in the same way as the lamp is an instrument for the electric current to express itself. All creation gives witness to God's presence and power.

There are areas on our Earth where the light of the sun is absent for several months each year. People who live there know that even if they cannot see the sun, it is there, beyond the horizon. We do not have to necessarily see something to believe in it. But if we believe, we shall experience the light of the soul in our inner being. God is light, the power in every manifestation of life in the entire universe. The universal life soul, God, is the spirit inherent in our true being. We have been seeking for God everywhere, except where He always has been, in our inner selves.

Our thoughts and our consciousness are our individual soul, indissoluble energy, that leaves the body in the hour of death. Our real I does not die in death, only the physical body dies. Our inner I only changes shape. Our thoughts, desires and wishes follow us. As we are on Earth, so we are also on the other side. Our thoughts are like an uninterrupted stream that follows us wherever we go.

Our soul enters a body of light. We go over to another form of life, where the limitless resources of life and the universe will be revealed to us in the light of our soul. In the state we then experience, we have no physical body that prevents us from seeing and hearing that which we could not, while living on Earth. It is said that sleep is the brother of death. When we lived on Earth and were sunk in deep sleep, our soul left the body to journey in the cosmos, to its primeval home. In the hour of death our life soul merges in the universal soul. The body dies, but our soul lives forever.

In the dimension in which we then exist we cannot escape anymore. The voice of our conscience speaks clearly. The unerring law of cause and effect (Karma) strikes back with the whole of its just power. When the oneness of all life is revealed in our consciousness, we understand that if we hurt others, we hurt God and hurt ourselves. By returning to Earth and entering a new physical body we can redeem our earlier wrong actions. Usually numerous reincarnations are needed before we succeed in liberating ourselves from the particular effects of our actions (Karma). This process does not come to an end until everything is redeemed.

Jesus taught us that we should not do to others what we do not want them to do to us. In these words Jesus warned us of the effects of the law of Karma.

Life and death are like the two sides of a coin. We cannot have one side without the other - the eternal pattern of the circle of life.

Heaven and Hell

An occultist lives a rich inner spiritual life, which is of greater importance than the external life. Consciousness is raised into a clearer light, grasps and understands more and more about the secrets of the universe. This is not an easy path, all cannot take to it. But one who has patience, a strong desire to live a spiritual life will be richly rewarded for his or her efforts. A deeper understanding is obtained that all creation follows universal cosmic laws. Also awareness comes that violation of these divine laws produces disharmony.

The good is harmonious, evil creates imbalance and disharmony. No person is entirely good, or entirely evil. Everything is relative. If we do allow the evil to develop, we create disharmony both in ourselves and in our surroundings. One who is truly intelligent and wise walks the path of love and light and has a better chance to avoid these pitfalls.

Evil exists as long as we succumb and allow it to govern our mind and senses. We can liberate ourselves from such a state of mind by the same means we created it. We are ourselves masters over our thoughts. A good man has good thoughts, an evil one has bad thoughts. For both good and bad, we are slaves to the power of our thoughts. We become what we think. In Dante's allegory "La Divina Commedia" ("The Divine Comedy"), those condemned to suffer in Hell represent people still living on Earth in his time but suffering a hellish existence. Similarly our consciousness can be in Heaven while our body is still on Earth. Jesus said, "Truly I say to you, you carry the kingdom of Heaven within." He could have added that we also carry Hell within. Through good, unselfish thoughts and deeds we can create a

Heaven on Earth for those, who are hard-stricken. Evil, on the contrary, can create a Hell. This we can clearly see daily, among other things in all the wars still being waged on our Earth.

Trials and sufferings come and go. We all have our burden to bear. It is said that nobody gets a heavier burden to carry than he or she can manage. Through ignorance we make mistakes. Therefore suffering has its cause in ignorance. We all are pupils in the school of life, which sometimes tests us in a hard way. The wise learn rapidly and do not repeat their faults. Suffering is a strong and just teacher.

I think it was the Chinese philosopher Confucius who said, "Through suffering our soul is disciplined and gives us the qualities we are lacking." The disciples of Jesus had to endure much ignominy and suffering because of their beliefs, but they were also entrusted with a great and important commission. Jesus said, "On you I shall build the gospels of the future."

Suffering is the consequence of our misdeeds committed in the past. Nobody is rid of their afflictions before they have gone through valleys of darkness. The law of karma, of cause and effect, does not fail.

A wise person has a clear perspective of his or her life and carries any burdens with equanimity. Success and misfortune have equal effect. If such a person suffers it is accepted that it is the consequence of wrong and imperfect thoughts and deeds of the past. Suffering is welcomed. It is known that one day the secret of suffering will have to be learnt. The bonds which tie us to this heavy yoke have their roots in selfishness of the ego. When full awareness is gained the goal of liberation has been reached and there is no longer need for fear of life or death.

One who practises meditation, and other spiritual exercises, has the goal to experience how the higher Self liberates itself from the lower self. A person, who is in this divine state, experiences the mergence in oneness, the realization of the cosmic consciousness. It is not given to many to reach the world of cosmic consciousness, and few are those who learn the hard lesson of suffering and life. Yet, one day we all shall reach the goal of liberation.

Life is a drama. God is the dramatist and the director. Every life on Earth means a new Act. The internal actor is always the same. Only the costume has changed to express the drama of the soul in a new part.

God Speaks Through His Chosen Prophets

The Vedic Scriptures are said to be the origin of all World Religions. During the passing of time new prophets have declared that they are God's messengers. They have laid the ground for various religions, which then have been developed in human hands and have been spread all over our Earth. God had revealed Himself to these holy men and given them divine directions to convey to all peoples on Earth.

Moses was a prophet and divine messenger. In The Old Testament it is told how he went up to Mount Sinai to pray. Here Moses heard God's voice advising him how he should lead the people of Israel out of Egypt. He received also moral guidance (the Ten Commandments) which the Hebrews were to follow. These Moses announced and explained to them. This is one of many examples how God has spoken to humankind through His chosen prophets to guide them.

Mohammed was a simple and pious man, he glorified and worshipped God. In a vision God revealed the way He had chosen for him. Then Mohammed announced God's message for the people of Arabia, which later was written down and constitutes the holy Koran. Millions of Muslims all over the world have taken these divinely inspired words to their heart. In their prayers and songs of praise they glorify and thank the Lord God for the divine messages they have received through their prophet Mohammed.

It is said that the Vedic Scriptures have originated in a similar way. In India Rishis, holy men, devoted their time and energy to spiritual yoga exercises. In the Himalayan mountains they sat engrossed in deep stillness and meditation. In their transcendental state of mind God spoke to them in their inner being. These divine messages constitute the essential basis of the Vedas.

God has given humanity these holy scriptures so that we are able to imbibe His message of love. Let us therefore approach God's wisdom with deep reverence and in our heart ponder over His love, which streams towards us through these divine writings. God is eternal, and so is His voice. Thus today God's voice can be heard and understood by mankind as in previous times.

Through yoga the Rishis had reached a superconscious state of trance, entirely enclosed in the pure divine consciousness. They experienced how their inner being merged in God's soul in the cosmos. In this superconscious state they heard God's voice speak and became aware of divine wisdom. The real creator of the divine voice they heard was the voice of their own divine pure consciousness. Through yoga and similar spiritual exercises the holy Rishis, Moses, Buddha, Jesus and others had learnt to free themselves from their lower I-consciousness through the power of thought. They could put themselves into a pure superconscious state of trance, where they merged in the consciousness of the cosmic existence. In the absolute stillness that then prevailed, they heard and comprehended the voice of the pure divine consciousness we call God.

This superconscious state of mind must not be compared with what we usually call meditation, where the voice of the ego speaks. This comes from our own lower world of thoughts, which is filled with worldly thoughts and desires, and therefore we hear what we want to hear. To believe that we hear the voice of our higher divine consciousness is not correct. It is created by our lower consciousness. How often do we hear that people think that God has spoken to them and requested them to commit actions that are inherently criminal. Afterwards they excuse themselves by declaring that it had been God's will that it should be done. Real meditation does not begin until one has entirely freed oneself from body consciousness and is no longer aware that one meditates.

Man's true nature is divine, perfect, and our soul is immortal, eternal. Spiritual exercises purify our thoughts and our consciousness, open the window of the soul towards God's light. In the brightness of that light we hear and see what we earlier could neither hear nor see, when our thoughts were under the influence of our lower self. We are a creation of Brahman's spirit and energy. Therefore the voice of our inner being is also divine pure consciousness, God's voice. The great scientist Einstein said, "What my intellect alone is unable to create comes from a higher level of divine consciousness." Einstein had the capacity to concentrate so intensively on the task at hand, that he could put himself into a state of cosmic pure consciousness, from where he could fetch the knowledge his brilliant intellect was unable to give him.

It is not unusual that scientists, artists, composers and other gifted persons have the ability to so entirely go into their task, that they are unconsciously lifted up to a higher level of consciousness. From there they get the inspiration and ability that enable them to create masterpieces and make scientific discoveries. Finland's greatest composer, Jean Sibelius, once took a ride by boat down the rapids of the Lule River. He was deeply sunk in his thoughts and experiences when sitting amidst the grand, powerful roaring of the rushing fall of waters. Suddenly Sibelius exclaimed in excitement, "I hear tones! I hear tones!" He became so entirely one with his creation in the world of music, that the roaring tones of the rapids inspired him to the greatest masterpiece he ever created, his world-famous composition "Finlandia."

The pure consciousness reveals what earlier had been hidden. Buddha sat seven years uninterruptedly under the shade of a tree and practised yoga-exercises to purify His consciousness. Not until He had reached the state of pure consciousness did He appear in public to reveal the wisdom He had acquired in His transcendental state of mind. Those years of meditation culminated in Buddha reaching Nirvana, the extinguishing of the lower self and merger in the higher cosmic consciousness. This gave Him the wisdom that is the basis of the Buddhist philosophy of life.

In a similar way Jesus spent many years, in the then secret monastery schools in India and Egypt, where He was initiated under the guidance of spiritual masters into the practice of yoga. Here Jesus developed those supernatural powers which He later demonstrated to His congregations. He had learnt to control the elements of nature, to perform all the miracles that are told about in the Bible.

In a similar way to Buddha and Jesus, other holy men, through daily practice of spiritual exercises, have come into possession of the spiritual powers, which they in their lives have been able to demonstrate. All of them had learnt to master their thoughts and the desires of the ego, which is a prerequisite for becoming able to reach a transcendental state of higher consciousness. To reach this state is not an easy task, as everybody knows who once has tried. In the Bhagavad Gita, ("The Song Of God"), a small part of the epic "Mahabharata," one of the most renowned epics of India, it is told how the Avạtar Krishna said to his friend and disciple Arjuna, "Arjuna, become a yogi!" He gave him advice how to practise various spiritual exercises, and Arjuna followed the instructions of his master. But after some time he returned to Krishna and complained, "Truly, it is easier to tame ten wild horses than to control the senses and become master over my thoughts." Arjuna was not inexperienced in the spiritual field but, despite this, he could not manage this difficult task. Not until Lord Krishna in His grace had taken over the guidance of his spiritual exercises could Arjuna succeed in becoming a yogi, a spiritual master and holy man.

Incarnation and Karma

The doctrine of reincarnation had once been proclaimed by all the great World Religions and is one of the oldest the history of religion knows. Even the Christian church had originally professed the validity of this doctrine, which Jesus confirmed when declaring that John the Baptist was a reincarnation of Elias. In Bhagavad Gita it is said that all the worlds, even the highest one, are subject to reincarnation. The Ancient Greek philosophers, Pythagoras, Plato and others, proclaimed that the human soul has again and again to be reborn in a new body, for further development.

There are many who find the doctrine of reincarnation difficult to comprehend, which is the reason for it appearing strange for so many. If one but takes the time and goes deeper into it, one will find it to be both fascinating, reasonable and intelligible. Many great thinkers in all times have declared that the soul does not die, it only changes. Goethe said that it is good for man to die, to have the impressions of each lifetime obliterated and then to come back to a new body.

Man's life on Earth is only a step which we take, to go forward and prepare ourselves for another earthly sojourn, as soon as we are prepared for gathering new experiences. The law of cause and effect teaches us that our life today is the result of what we thought and did in the past. The fruits of our life are the consequence of our own deeds in this or an earlier life.

One who correctly understands the doctrine of rebirth of the soul finds answers to many of life's problems. The great goal is to learn to know our inner self and to understand the meaning of our own lives as well as the ultimate Truth. Socrates, who is called the master of intellect, gave the following answer to one of his disciples who had asked what is the most important thing to be learnt in life. "Learn to know yourself and you learn to know God." Our real self is the life soul we call God, in our inner being.

God has given humankind the capacity for rational thinking. Therefore we are conscious beings. God has also given us a free will to determine our thoughts and deeds. We ourselves decide whether we want to use the creative capacity of thought in service of the good or its opposite. We have ourselves to bear the consequences of our actions. We cannot blame God and make Him responsible for what we think and do. Nor can we say, "How could God allow this evil, which has caused so much suffering, to happen?" God has not requested us to commit bad deeds. Through our free will we ourselves have chosen our way. It is untenable and absurd to make the cosmic creative energy we call God responsible for our actions. We become what we think.

Through karma, the law of cause and effect, we have to harvest what we have sown. If we sow good thoughts in the soil of our mind, we shall reap good fruits. Our destiny is a consequence of the karma that we from life to life have woven through our thoughts and actions. There are no coincidences or mystic powers involved, it is we who reward or punish ourselves. Our life today determines the nature of our next life on Earth. We hold our destiny in our own hands. We have a free will to use, through our intellect and ability. We ourselves have created the past as well as the present, and our future depends on what direction we give it during this life. Buddha said, "We are the result of what we have thought." The French philosopher Jean Paul Sartre expressed it the other way by saying, "We are the sum of our actions."

There is a clear, inevitable connection between cause and effect. Our character crystallizes and creates our karma. The effect is the child of the cause, they go hand in hand. We have the seed within us of what we shall have to go through. Our thoughts are living beings that create our future fate. God does not choose for us, we ourselves choose the way we shall have to go.

In the Vedas it is said that all life in the entire universe was once a divine thought. Man is the child of creation. Our thoughts bind us to the divine Presence within, as well as to cosmic consciousness. What we determined and wholeheartedly think of, that we shall reach. The power of our thoughts creates what we desire, both on the spiritual and on the material plane.

If we believe that our true inner being is divine, we shall one day experience that we are Gods in a human body, through which God expresses Himself. Two thousand years ago Jesus said the same as Sai Baba today keeps reminding us, "You are Gods, but you do not know it." Jesus said, "Truly I do tell you, you all are Gods."

When we say that we love God, it must include all living beings, friends as well as foes, as God dwells in all creation. All is one. Therefore we must not divide God as it suits us. We must not say that we love our friend, but not our enemy, as little as we should say that we love only part of nature. We experience both people and nature in different ways, but that does not prevent us from feeling love for God who dwells in all creation. One who is aware of the divine oneness is also aware that if we injure part of this oneness, even the minutest creeping creature, we injure God, we injure ourselves. The great champion of freedom and love, Mahatma Gandhi, always took a careful look before he sat down somewhere or took a step. He didn't want to injure any living being. He knew that God is the inner core of both big and small.

Our way of becoming God-conscious beings is for most of us still long and laborious. It usually comprises many more lives on Earth. Therefore it is so important for us to take our steps in the right direction, so that we one day shall reach the goal of fulfilment and liberation. Jesus said, "Seek, and you shall find. Go into your chamber and pray to the Father in private, and He will give you what you ask for." By "in private" Jesus meant our inner nature.

The power of the spirit is great. What we wholeheartedly desire, think of and ask for, that we create. Wishes and thoughts put forces into action which cannot be stopped. Therefore we ought to be careful for what we wish. For the spiritual seeker the world loses its lustre little by little, and personal desires fade and cease the more our thoughts are engaged in spiritual values.

Within us there is the spring of all knowledge. If we shut out the world around us, reach a state of stillness and harmony with the divine Presence, our soul is lifted up to a higher plane, liberated from the ego-consciousness. The voice of silence can be heard. We hear the inaudible and see the invisible, which earlier were hidden from us. Divine wisdom manifests itself. Consciousness that God and Truth are within us are experienced from the soul's journey in the cosmos.

When we reach the depth of contemplation we are no longer aware of meditating. Our consciousness has reached a higher world, where we experience oneness with the universal consciousness. Exactly how this has happened, how we became conscious about the information we have been given on this higher plane, is not easy to explain with either intellect or science. We have listened to and understood what has been revealed for us when the soul had opened the window towards light and the world of cosmic consciousness, which is the same as to experience God. In that transcendental state God has revealed Himself for us in love and light, and we have through our own divine pure consciousness been able to listen to His voice.

Human kind has been fighting about esoteric truths as long as religions have existed. Those who think they know, mostly do not know, but nevertheless warn against false prophets. In their own ignorance they warn against those who have reached a higher knowledge. What one does not know and understand seems often strange and dangerous. God is too great, too all-embracing for our limited intellect to understand. Sai Baba says, "How shall the limited be able to understand the limitless?" Only on the higher level of consciousness can we get a glimpse of God's infinity.

Victory Over Our Ego

Both will power and courage are needed to gain a lasting victory over oneself. To conquer our ego we must dare to see and be able to acknowledge ourselves as we are. The great thinker and philosopher Swedenborg was not too great to admit his weaknesses and to accept his set-backs were due to mistakes he had made. If we cannot realize that it is our ego that misleads us, we bind ourselves with our own bonds until we have learnt to understand that our wrong thoughts have led us to the wrong deeds we have committed.

If we searched in our inner consciousness, in the depth of the soul, we would learn to know the truth about ourselves that could lift us out of the darkness of ignorance which has distorted our view of life. When we can confess that our imperfect thoughts have been the cause for our wrong actions, we have taken a large step towards liberation from the ego.

Yearning to know our origin has engaged man's mind ever since we became thinking, conscious beings. This yearning is our desire to return to our source. The material world in which we live today has more and more separated us from our inner reality and consciousness of our origin. May the divine light of our soul lead us back from unreality to reality.

Those who show interest in the spiritual world are today looked down upon. They are regarded as impractical and separated from reality, dreamers who live in the world of imagination. Today it is more important to devote one's time and energy to becoming successful in the material world. What counts is quantity, not quality. In such a world no spirituality can flourish. Were we but more conscious of the meaning of life, we would approach a spiritually developed person with reverence.

Those who have a pure heart love silence, for there God has His abode. Those who wander along the path of silence are heading for wisdom. Many spiritually enlightened persons have gone silent through life. During my stay with Sai Baba I read some stanzas written by the Indian saint Kabir. This highly gifted poet, once a humble weaver, said, "I have turned away from the world, have forgotten my family and caste. Now I'm weaving in infinite silence. In silence I have found God within myself."

To conquer the voice of the senses, the flights of thought, to hear God speak, can only be achieved by one who has patience and a sincere desire to know God in one's inner being. Many have had a long life, but have never taken the time to listen to God who tried to make His voice heard in the temple of the heart.

We carefully try to keep our body clean, but we easily forget the purity of our heart. A great thinker has said, "The light of the lamp burns clear and bright when both wick and oil are pure. Therefore, do not let the wick darken the glass of your lamp." May the lamp of our soul always shine clearly on the way we have to go, so that we do not lose sight of the meaning and goal of our life.

A strong yearning for Truth, belief in and love for God, purifies our heart, liberates us from the illusory world of the ego and enables us to love beyond all limits. The day we have learnt to live in accordance with Sai Baba's teachings, live in love and peace with each other, we have taken an important step nearer to realization of our divine true Self.

Meditation

One day Sai Baba was instructing a group of His older college students in the difficult art of meditation and asked me to be present. On an earlier occasion, described in the trip to Ooty, Sai Baba had asked me to tell His students about my method of meditation. Now I had the great pleasure to hear the master of all yogis, Sai Baba Himself, teach.

Sai Baba says there are three steps: concentration, contemplation and meditation. When contemplation is deepened it quite naturally develops into meditation. The last mentioned cannot be enforced, it develops naturally. If one who meditates is aware of himself and that he is meditating, then he does not meditate.

Meditation is beyond all sense perceptions. In the state of meditation one is only conscious of the object of meditation. Finally one identifies oneself entirely and becomes one with the object. This is real meditation, beyond body consciousness.

For those who wish to take up meditation practices, Sai Baba recommends as a first step to pacify one's thoughts. This is best done by repeating words to the glory of God. By repeating God's name, allow the form which is represented by the name you use, to arise before your inner sight. If your thoughts wander away from God's name, lead them back to God's form. If you cannot retain concentration on the form, lead your thoughts back to the name. Let your thoughts dwell on both God's name and God's form.

If we treat our thoughts in this way, we can learn to control them. Little by little the conceptual picture will be transformed into an emotional picture, which becomes deeply rooted in our consciousness. Finally God takes this form, to fulfil our desire.

For beginners Sai Baba recommends this form of meditation, concentration on God's name and form. In this way one learns to control one's thoughts and senses.

In silence and stillness the Pranava AUM can be heard in our inner being. It is the sound which was created by the first movement of cosmic energies. AUM is the primeval, basic sound out of which all sounds and all languages have developed. Therefore AUM is the symbol for the universal absolute.

When we have learnt to master meditation on God's name and form we are ready for meditation on the holy mantra AUM. AUM must be pronounced as slowly as possible and must result in a crescendo, thereafter dying down and becoming part of the stillness that vibrates in our heart. This resonance coincides with and merges in the vibrations of the entire universe. The power of these vibrations evokes the consciousness of the formless Presence of God in our inner being, and we become one with the cosmic consciousness.

If we dive deep into the stillness, we can hear the cosmic AUM with which the universe is filled. In this state we can experience how our inner true being merges in the cosmic oversoul, God.

I have followed the advice Sai Baba gave me about spiritual practices in order to attain unity with the universal consciousness, God.

In 1980 during our lengthy stay in India I was able to provide some information about my meditation which was published in Sanathana Sarathi, the Ashram magazine from Puttaparthi, as well as Bob Lowenberg's book, "The Heart Of Sai." I wanted to share my experiences so that others may have similar opportunities to experience the deeper levels and meaning of life that Sai Baba is trying to teach us. Some of the notes in those publications have been described elsewhere in this book, but it is appropriate that I expand on aspects of meditation here.

I meditated on SO-HAM, the sound that ensues from our inhaling and exhaling breath. If we listen carefully, we can hear our breathing repeating the sound SO-HAM. Translated this means I-He, 'we are one.' Initially, when Sai Baba instructed me to meditate on SO-HAM, it was only words, as yet I did not understand the significance. But naturally there was no hesitation to follow the advice and to meditate on the real meaning. Over these several years the significance of SO-HAM has become a living reality of the creating and life-maintaining power of God's presence in my heart.

I also meditated on the light, and experienced that I was the light. I experienced oneness with the light in the cosmos, I was one with the light and the creating power. He was I, I was He. We were one. I experienced the unity as an answer to my yearning for learning to know God, the Truth, His omnipresent creating power. I will describe some experiences which brought this realization to fruition.

Before I sit for meditation I pray, "God, lead me from darkness to light, from the unreal to the real, from death to immortality." I ask that He in His love and divine wisdom may cleanse my consciousness, so that I shall understand and be able to experience the divine truth which God is revealing when I am sitting enveloped in His love and light.

In the earlier years I then continued with a pattern. The first stage was to concentrate on God in my heart and visualize God's form. I kept a picture of the physical form of Sai Baba for about fifteen to twenty minutes in my inner vision. Then I felt great happiness in my heart, and at the same time sank deeper and deeper into the next stage, contemplation. I felt the presence of God very strongly as well as a deep inner peace. At that stage I transferred my concentration to an object of spiritual nature and retained it there. This allowed me to see the object in a deeper and clearer light. In this way the intellect became sharpened and I saw the object even more clearly. Intuitively I understood the meaning of the mental form which has been created, in other words, the essence of my previous knowledge ripened to wisdom, guided by intuition.

From this point, which I would like to define as the border state, I then reached the deepest phase of meditation. Here the concentration becomes strengthened and I entered an absolute stillness. Often I felt strong vibrations in my body, and a clear light formed around me, especially around my breast and head. I experienced a bright light in the form of a beam, emanating from the so-called third eye region.

Surrounded by this divine light, I then lose all sense of space and time. This light takes my soul on a voyage in the cosmos, which the scriptures call the individual soul merging with the cosmic soul. The experiences in the cosmos are registered by the super-conscious so that they are retained in the conscious part of my brain. In this way I become fully aware of these divine visions, which also give me divine knowledge. All this I understand after awakening from the state of meditative trance.

In one of these states of deep yoga trance I was taken on the beam of light emanating from between my eye-brows into the cosmos. Powerful sound waves were echoing the sound AUM in the cosmos. I became part of these sound waves. As though by telepathic transfer I understood the language of the sound waves. A bright light took form in the cosmos, a rosy-white, impossible to adequately describe in words. My super-consciousness formed a question, "What is this?" The cosmic voice in the light answered, "It is I, God!"

At that very moment I was fully conscious of God. I experienced God and comprehended His true nature. I saw a personage take form in the light - I caught a glimpse of a picture of Sai Baba, so very dear to me. My soul trembled. The voice in the light echoed throughout the universe, "All you experience is Me. I am the cosmic power."

The question came to me, "Is this light Your soul?". The answer was, "Yes!" I continued, "How does my soul look?". Before my question was even fully formed a small streak of light, being the same colour as the great light, appeared. After a moment the small streak of light merged into the great one. God was no longer visible, but I heard His voice, "You see, we are one. I give you divine wisdom." Slowly I returned to consciousness. An indescribable peace and stillness, combined with a bright light, surrounded me again.

Through Sai Baba's divine guidance my meditation has more and more deepened. As I only need two to three hours sleep each night I rise early, before the sunrise, to sit for meditation. As soon as I have sat down I experience the intensity of the light so strongly both within and outside of my1 body, that my soul leaves my body on the rays of the light to merge in God's light and cosmic pure energy.

In the depths of our soul there is God, our inner reality. The way to truth is through our soul. God is truth. God is love. God is light.

In His grace God has let me experience the truth in the words Sai Baba once wrote to me, "I shall give you all the blessings you are asking for." These words I have always with gratitude and love kept living in my heart. Sai Ram! - What we with love and a pure heart ask God for, that we shall one day receive.

Through God's grace I am conscious that my inner reality is not separate from Brahman, God's soul, the creating and maintaining power in the entire universe. All life, all forms, are His. There is only one God!

This is the truth that God has revealed to me, when my soul, my consciousness, in meditation has been enveloped in God's cosmic, pure consciousness. Our true I (Self) is cosmic consciousness, God!

In love and deep reverence I bow down at Sai Baba's Divine Lotus Feet, in humble gratitude that He in His grace has let me experience this divine truth.

Wisdom

To adequately define wisdom is nearly as difficult as describing God. Both have been and are expressed in so many different ways, depending on the various circumstances that prevail. They are interpreted in accordance with the capacity of the individual person. Those who think they know what the essential nature of wisdom is, say that it is the crystallized essence of knowledge, experience and intuition. But is this the whole truth?

One who can truly be called wise is characterized by humility. Whereas one who possesses knowledge in various fields is often proud and egotistically shows off skills. Bookish knowledge says so little. There are many who read much, but few who think. Schools, universities and other learning institutions offer knowledge of various kinds. If one has time, economic resources and is normally gifted, without great difficulty it is possible to acquire knowledge in the most varied fields. Wisdom, on the other hand, is seldom to be found in the confines of universities, it has to be searched for elsewhere.

There is a considerable difference between what educational institutions offer and real wisdom. One can master ten different languages, but it does not necessarily mean that one has something wise to say. The book-learned person feels secure within the bounds of his or her field of learning, relying upon such acquired knowledge. Problems lying outside this domain result in confusion, as a solution cannot be found in the world of books.

On the other hand a wise person does not need to rely upon acquired knowledge. Answers are derived from a more reliable source. The wise have learnt to search within, where the answers to the questions of life can be found. Mankind carries within the ability to obtain the answers to all the secrets of life and the universe. If we but take the time to search for what lies hidden in the treasury of our own subconscious and dive deep enough into this spring of wisdom, we can discover the most precious pearls of divine wisdom.

Meditation sharpens our senses, the power of intuition awakens into life and the clear flame of wisdom is lit in our inner being. The spiritually minded seek to find clarity about the secrets of life and the universe. They have learnt to shut out the illusory world, to quieten the mind and tune in the consciousness to the correct wave length. Then the signals of cosmic consciousness can be perceived and interpreted. We have the capacity to both send and receive thought vibrations, which in our subconsciousness are formed into clear pictures. From there the wise can acquire knowledge which is hidden for others. Our thoughts are energies which can never be dissolved. They are forever stored in the data bank of our subconsciousness and are picked up by the cosmic consciousness.

We must pay careful attention to what we think. The wise have learnt to think with responsibility and love. Often they retire from the world and follow the motto of the sphinx, "To know, to will, to dare and to be silent."

The aim of knowledge is love
The aim of education is character
The aim of wisdom is freedom

A Divine Dream Vision

God has many ways to guide and help us. He comes to us in the form which each of us can best comprehend and interpret. He speaks to us through our intuition and inspiration, in our feelings and presentiments, our ideas and impulses. God reveals Himself in bliss and peace in our heart. Sometimes it happens that He reveals Himself for us in visions, when our I-consciousness is enclosed in a deepened God-consciousness. God also reveals Himself to us in our dreams.

Through God's grace a few years ago I experienced a vision in which I was wandering along a street in a strange country. The people I met had the appearance of Southern Europeans. At a distance I saw a group of men standing bent over something that was lying on the ground. When I came nearer I could see that it was a large bird lying there helpless.

The wings of the bird were covered with a layer of brownish, dirty clay. On closer inspection I found out that it was an eagle with the typical strong, bent beak. I could see that its eyes were sharp and piercing. It made desperate efforts to move its wings, but could not because of the sticky covering of clay. The men standing around did not dare to touch the bird, but stayed at a safe distance. They were all afraid of its sharp beak, that could have easily bitten off a finger.

I felt deep sympathy and love for the helpless bird on the ground. Without hesitation I bent down and cautiously stroked its wings. I had only one thought, to free this creature from its captivity.

The bird lay entirely still and let itself be treated by me. It understood that I was trying to free it. The men around expressed their astonishment and admiration for my courage and determination. In fact, I had been as afraid as they, but was motivated by my strong inner feeling at the sight of the bird.

After a while my work began to show its effect. The bird stretched out its wings and freed itself from the rest of its covering. It turned its head towards me and gave me a grateful look, rose up, fluttered its wings a few times, before it flew up in the air above our heads. A murmur of happiness was heard from the men, when the large bird rose towards the sky. My eyes were filled with tears, my heart was full of happiness. The bird turned back, circled a few times above us, before it disappeared, its wings beating strongly.

In my vision I felt intuitively that the eagle symbolized myself, and therefore I had without hesitation interfered. I was myself bound by the illusory desires of the ego, from which I wanted fervently to free myself by all possible means.

God had interfered, had given me this vision and thereby made me conscious of my own situation. I understood that I should not waste any time. I should immediately intervene and begin the necessary inner purification process.

A difficult task lay ahead of me, but I was firmly determined to immediately begin the work to liberate myself from the bonds of the ego. I prayed to Sai Baba to guide my steps away from the illusory world to which I had been bound, and lead me from darkness into light. "Help me to see clearly, purify my thoughts and my senses. Let me become conscious of Your omnipresence and experience the divine oneness in all creation."

I understood that only through God's grace and blessing could I reach purification and liberation. Thus, like the bird in the symbolic vision, I could obtain strength to lift myself into a clearer and purer consciousness, liberated from the bonds of the ego that had kept me imprisoned and prevented my spiritual development.

Not until I had experienced this vision of the helpless bird could I understand the entire significance of Sai Baba's blessing, when He had laid His hand on my head and said, "I shall give you a special blessing and take away the darkness from your eyes."

I had not previously been ready to follow the path that now lay before me. I had not understood how to control my thoughts, my desires. By my own efforts I had not been able to free myself from my selfishness, my ego. Only God could help me to liberate myself from the illusions of the ego.

God had given me this vision so that I should understand how bound I was by my selfish thoughts. Now I was ready and could begin the important and necessary purification work. I am humbly grateful and happy that God in His love and grace gave me this divine dream vision, which made me conscious about the truth about myself.

Dear Sai Baba,
Give me power and intellect to change what I in my selfish ignorance have created.
Give me strength to overcome my weaknesses.
Give me humility and a contented heart.
Let Your divine light show me the way to the goal of liberation.
Give me a loving heart which mirrors Your divine mercy.
Give me intellect to become conscious about the divine Truth.
Give me the ability to love and live in love.
Speak, my Lord, when I have to speak, so that Your divine love and wisdom can be expressed in my words and deeds.
Let Your will be mine.

Visions

We all have sometimes experienced how we have become immersed in our thoughts and allowed ourselves to be led by our innermost wishes. Our day-dream visions can contain everything, wealth, fame and honour, journeys and adventures, good fortune and joy, a long and happy life. The list of wishes and day-dreams is endless. Our wishes create our day-dream visions, take form in visionary pictures.

Our dreams during *the light sleep* phase are often influenced by happenings and thoughts, which have recently engaged our mind. Usually we can trace the connection. Even if the dream pictures are distorted, we find in our dreams a clear pattern corresponding to what we in our day consciousness have experienced.

In the dream vision of *the deep sleep* phase we have left body consciousness and thereby freed ourselves from our desires and wishes. Our dream world is not always so easy to understand and interpret. When we wake up after a dream we have often diffuse memories of what we dreamt. Only disconnected pictures remain in our memory, which make it difficult to understand or interpret our dreams. When we cannot give them a meaningful content and value, we push them aside.

Psychologists, who specialize in this field, teach us how to better remember our dreams and interpret their significance. Their advice is that, before falling asleep, we should give a determined instruction to our subconscious, and when awakening we will better remember what we dreamt. After some weeks of practising this technique we should notice an improvement. We remember our dreams better and clearer. Our subconscious has preserved the contents of our dreams in clearer pictures.

It may sometimes happen that our dreams take a very concrete form. The dream has given us a vision of something that has just happened or will happen in future. On awakening we have a clear memory picture of what we in our dream vision experienced. In common parlance we call them *dreams that come true*. Our subconscious, that recognizes and knows everything, has in the dream opened the world that in day-consciousness usually is hidden from us.

Many people have verified their true dreams by clear evidence. What happens in the dream is exactly what has happened or will happen in reality. The genuineness of dream visions is clearly documented by extensive research work. The deeper the sleep is, the more distant is our body consciousness.

Our thoughts, which are the cause of our actions, are creating energies which get caught up by the cosmic consciousness. They can never be dissolved, they are stored for eternity in the cosmic data bank. All we thought and did during our collected earthly sojourns is preserved here. Our thoughts do not get dissolved just because we no longer remember what we earlier thought. The cosmic consciousness is a reality, though we are not aware of it.

What prevents us from getting in touch with the cosmic consciousness is the strong constraint of our body consciousness. We cannot like the yogi free ourselves from our lower I-consciousness. Only in deep sleep do we leave our body consciousness and we can, under favourable conditions, experience and retain the memory of a true dream vision.

It happens that a thought from our subconscious rises up to the surface of our day-consciousness. A thought that we long ago have forgotten is remembered in all its clarity, when we least of all anticipated it. Maybe it is something good we once did, but it can also be a thought that fills us with pain and sorrow, which we most of all had wished to forget forever. It can have happened a long time ago, but now suddenly the memory again becomes vivid in the mind's eye. Our subconscious does not forget!

Hundreds' of thousands of years ago mankind's thought capacity began to develop. Consequently we are today conscious beings. This makes it possible for us to experience true dreams and visions. Our consciousness and subconsciousness are a unity which is not dissolved and does not die with our body. It goes on living, in due time taking possession of a different body for a new period of earthly life, a further period of development. Our consciousness is our life soul which follows us from life to life and is not separated from the cosmic consciousness.

In the dream world of sleep it is our subconscious self that creates our visions and gives us our factual dreams. Our subconscious knows the past, therefore we can in the dream world of sleep obtain a clear vision of reality. The yogi who has learnt to control his senses does not need to utilize the dream world of sleep to experience a clear vision. In his superconscious state of trance he is one with the cosmic consciousness and can see into the past as well as into the future.

A yogi has learnt to concentrate his thoughts and free himself from body consciousness. In this state he sinks deeper into the ocean of stillness and silence, beyond time and space. Through his will he has put himself into the transcendental state of superconsciousness which lies beyond the limits of the world of the senses. Nothing is hidden from the inner sight of a yogi. In his superconscious state he is able to freely move his consciousness in time and space, he is one with the universal consciousness which gives him visions of God's reality.

When the yogi is in a state of trance, his pure consciousness reaches the kernel of the cosmic consciousness, where he obtains all the knowledge he wishes. This is possible because his consciousness has reached the vibration frequency of the cosmic consciousness. In other words, he has managed to tune in his consciousness to the gathered knowledge that since the beginning of time has been stored in the cosmic consciousness.

Nothing is hidden from us, but we must learn to liberate ourselves from our senses. We must dive deep into the stillness and silence to be able to benefit from the wisdom which is the essence of humanity's thoughts since the beginning of time and which has been preserved in the cosmic consciousness.

Those who have learnt to completely control their senses and the power of thought can after awakening preserve the memory of the transcendental experiences received during deep unity with the cosmic consciousness. They have a clear picture of the vision pure superconsciousness has given. This is the cause for being able to predict what will happen in future.

The present is the fruit of thoughts and deeds in the past, and in the present lie the seeds for all that will happen to us in the future.

Creation

Space, the absolute, was a still and lifeless void. Eternal darkness prevailed. Out of the void light appeared. How could emptiness bring forth light? Scientists as well as philosophers have come to the same conclusion: during countless years gas had been formed in space. This gas became extremely dense, until it suddenly exploded through its inherent power of compression. This is the momentous happening, called "The Big Bang" by scientists.

The number of solar systems that took form in the universe at that time is only an assumption. It is believed that there are millions of solar systems in outer space. This gives us some idea of the infinity of space. As a consequence of this cosmic explosion light manifested, and the creation of the universe had begun. Light is the ultimate cause for the formation of matter. Out of light was born the power which in the five thousand years old Vedic Scriptures is called Brahman. Therefore Brahman's primeval power is considered to be the supreme, highest creator of life in the universe.

Whether we call this primeval power Brahman, Divine Presence, God or give it other names, it is the same conception we talk about. Man can be called by many names, but his identify does not change thereby.

Out of the substance of light, the spirit, and the energy of Brahman were born. Brahman's power became more and more evident. It manifested itself in more and more various forms of life. The sun, the moon, the stars in the firmament, like the planet Earth, are His handiwork. Without the power of Brahman nothing could have been created. Through His divine energy the universe exists. Wherever and in whatever form it is manifested, it is the same. The spirit of Brahman incarnated itself in Deities as well as in man, and therefore Jesus, by force of His divine consciousness, could say, "My Father and I are one." We are all manifestations of God, we are all God's children.

Those who have reached a higher consciousness understand that it is God's powe that works through and enlightens them. We are human instruments through whom God expresses Himself. When the mind is stilled through yoga, we can experience the pure divine consciousness and how the soul in supreme bliss merges in the universal soul Brahman. We cannot see the soul of Brahman, but we feel His power that is manifested in our heart. The veil of ignorance hides the reality and makes us believe that we are separate. In reality our inner being is one with the primeval force of Brahman.

All beings are Brahman. The various divine forms appear to be different, but they are, nevertheless, one. Brahman is limited when manifested in various forms of life, but His true being is unlimited. He is in Himself as well as in man's pure consciousness. His supreme soul is mankind's soul.

God is eternally creating energy that constantly transforms itself into new forms of life, which we daily see in nature around us. Man is no exception to this life process. Our soul is immortal energy that manifests itself in new body forms when we again incarnate on Earth. All life follows the same pattern of renewal.

The sun is the life-giving spring of energy on our planet, the ultimate cause and condition for the development of life on our Earth. Millions of years after the first signs of life on Earth became visible, Brahman's power took form in microscopic, insignificant amoeba. This tiny, slimy, insignificant being is the origin of mankind. It has taken many millions of years and innumerable forms of life for the amoeba to develop to what science calls "homo sapiens," a being walking upright on two legs. From this stage of development hundreds of thousands of years had to pass before we became thinking, conscious beings.

When our brain had developed and we had thereby acquired the capacity of independent, conscious thought activity, fear was born in our consciousness. Mankind then pondered deeply over the question what that mystic power was that made land arise from the depths of the seas. This divine energy is the soul of nature, which expresses itself in the eternal development of life. It gave mankind the necessities for maintenance of life, but at the same time it was also in a frightening way present in catastrophes, which at that time were common phenomena. In a few moments these could lay waste what earlier had been created.

People, who could not understand and interpret the so-called outbreaks of nature's wrath, began to fear this mystic power they called God. They offered sacrificial gifts for appeasing the wrath of God, which they sometimes experienced as so awe-inspiring and terrifying that they even offered human lives. During the passing of time, what has not been offered on this altar! Mankind felt helpless in God's hands, dependent on His grace or suffering His punishment.

Since that time thousands of years have passed, and the intellect of mankind, the capacity for independent thought activity, has developed. In the material field we have made great progress, as the various sciences can prove. But morally and spiritually we are still on a low level of development.

It is said that the human mind is like the waves of the ocean. On the surface there is a terrible agitation, but in the depth of the ocean there is calmness. As long as our mind is restless we cannot experience our true nature. Our limited intellect limits our spiritual progress.

When we have through meditation and other spiritual exercises become masters over our senses, then that which our intellect was not capable of revealing, is revealed to us. Mankind possesses great worldly knowledge, but does not know his real nature. We have no peace in our heart. We search for happiness and a remedy for the vicissitudes of nature in the worldly, the temporary. A God-conscious man has lasting peace and happiness in his heart. Self-knowledge is to recognize God in all the diversity around us. We must break the confusing bonds of the senses and become conscious that our true nature is divine.

The Resources of the Earth are Given for Us All

Without the sun, the life spring of our Earth, the Earth would still be today a lifeless planet in the cosmos. The sun and the moon are examples of how the cosmic elemental forces influence human beings in both a positive and negative way. Nature transforms and renews itself constantly, which is a condition for our existence. The survival and development of man is entirely dependent on natural resources of our Earth. The land and the seas have since the beginning of time provided for us the necessities for living. We have become used to regarding these gifts of nature as a matter of course.

To the negative, destructive side of the elemental forces belong the innumerable catastrophes which time after time strike our Earth in the form of, for instance, earthquakes and floods. Similarly, destructive periods of drought have transformed green fruitful areas into desert. One example is the Sahara Desert which had once blooming, fruitful soils.

Millions of people have for thousands of years been hit by devastating catastrophes, resulting in extreme privations, suffering and death. Man cannot master the cosmic forces that influence our Earth. In his powerlessness mankind has directed prayers to God and asked for help from these merciless calamities. In spite of his prayers these misfortunes struck our Earth time and time again. Without understanding the causes for calamities, mankind believed that it was God's punishment for his sins and therefore laid the guilt on hmself for these outbursts of cosmic forces.

The cosmic force is omnipresent, is one and the same energy that gave and maintains life in our body. We apparently have little capacity to influence this life force where, when and in whatever form it may express itself on our Earth. All life is divine. The creating life energy follows its own laws, which, despite the sometimes negative effects, have been a great blessing for our existential development. We have to accept that this cosmic power is not always in the harmony and balance that we human beings wish.

It is said that life slumbers in the stone, awakens in the plant, moves in the animal and thinks in man. Man stands highest on the ladder of development and is called the crown of creation.

We can hardly deny that we live today in a dark and evil world. We are ourselves responsible for this. Had we but spent a little more time in reflection about our chosen direction, we would have a long time ago found another way. This would have led to a better and happier world for all people on our Earth to live in.

The root of this evil lies in our selfishness. When people stagnate in their spiritual development, all moral concepts diminish. Were we but more conscious about the real values of life, our selfishness would no longer have free scope to dominate the stage of life. The first step that can lead us to a brighter and more loving world is to admit that it is our egos' desire for power that has governed our actions. This has devastated the resources of our Earth. We are well on the way to annihilating both ourselves and the Earth we live on. We all must shoulder the responsibility, wake up and immediately start working for a sounder quality of life, so that our children and coming generations shall be able to live and develop in a harmonious and righteous world.

We must not forget that the resources of the Earth are given to all. The Earth is a home for all living beings. We human beings have a moral responsibility to aid the Earth to develop according to its own laws. We have no right to devastate and annihilate what we have inherited and must pass on to future generations. The resources of Earth have been placed in our trust for as long as we live here. Therefore we must be conscious of our responsibility and administer properly this precious treasure, which is a condition for life for all living beings.

Through divine providence the Earth has been given to us so that we should all be able to live and develop in an abundant and sustaining environment. Let us show greater gratitude and respect for the gift God has given us, than has been previously demonstrated by our actions. Our behaviour does not justify our being called the crown of creation! Only through transforming ourselves, by living more selflessly and by respecting life, God, in all forms, can we hope to succeed in restoring the balance of nature on Earth.

God is Omnipresent

An Avatar is a manifestation, an embodiment of God in human form on Earth. What a great blessing for us all that God in His love has incarnated amongst us as Sathya Sai Baba!

God is everywhere. He is always with us, in us. But if we have the opportunity to visit Sai Baba, it is a wonderful divine gift. Many are those who, like me, can testify that a personal meeting with and nearness to Sai Baba are immensely elevating experiences. I remember with warmth and gratitude the bliss I experienced every time, when coming into the sphere of His divine radiation of love and light. These divine meetings with Sai Baba have given me invaluable guidance in my spiritual development. His love consolidated the consciousness that He is always with me, wherever I may be, and that His love reaches out beyond all boundaries of time and space.

For meeting and learning to know Sai Baba we travel from all around the world to Puttaparthi. Were we but aware of His true nature, His omnipresence, we would understand that we can meet and experience Him everywhere and that He is not limited to His physical form in Puttaparthi.

Sai Baba knows that He is God, that each one of us also is God. What separates us from Him is our limited consciousness about this truth. What can be more important for us than becoming conscious of our divinity, our real Self?

If we were aware that our physical body is only a temporary abode for our divine inner Self, an instrument for God to express Himself through, then we would not identify ourselves with the body. It is important for us to liberate ourselves from this limitation and expand our consciousness. If we could do this we would be free, whenever we so desire, to be near Sai Baba and sit at His divine Lotus Feet. The day we possess this clear consciousness we do not need to move our physical body to various places on Earth to experience the presence of Sai.

Meditation is a way that can lead us to consciousness of God's presence within us and everywhere outside us. When through meditation we have learnt to free ourselves from body-consciousness, we reach a state of trance that gives us a divine super-consciousness. When our consciousness, our soul, is no longer bound to the body, we can with our divine will and the power of thought move our inner self anywhere we wish to be. One moment we are sitting sunk in meditation, in our home, the next we are in our divine consciousness at Prasanthi Nilayam at the Lotus Feet of Bhagavan Baba and having His darshan.

We must widen and purify our consciousness for seeing and experiencing God in all His multi-coloured, innumerable manifestations in nature, in all forms of life.

We are all treading the same path. Nobody is standing still in his spiritual development. Nobody is more divine than another. What makes the difference is the level of our spiritual development, our consciousness. For our spiritual growth during earthly life the most important task is to learn to know ourselves, our inner true divine Self.

Purposefully and wholeheartedly I have been searching for the Truth hiding behind the phenomenal world. The glimpses of Truth, that I have been given during my meditation, seem to me today more and more clearly as only fragments and a step towards the ultimate reality, the absolute Truth, God. The divine reality expresses itself in innumerable ways, so that very few can say, "I know the full Truth."

My Conception of God

I have asked myself, "Who am I? From where do I come? Who is the God I'm praying to and where do I go the day my life here on Earth ends?" I have also asked, "Is God a cosmic universal creating power, an energy that manifests itself in all creation? Is God the power that streams through the whole of my being?" And I asked further, "Could any form of life exist without being in combination with a universal life energy?"

I have thought much about these questions and thereby become conscious that God is the universal energy in all the millions of various forms of creation that exist in the boundless universe. I come from God, my true nature is divine and one day I shall return to my source, God. God is life. I think there is also life on other planets in the universe, but in different forms.

We human beings are part of the oneness of the divine creation. In reality we are one, but through our ignorance we are not aware of it. What makes the difference between ordinary people and Sai Baba is His divine pure consciousness. Sai Baba knows that He is God, that He in no way differs from the creating force of the divine life energy. They are identical concepts.

Through Sai Baba's love and grace my consciousness has been lifted into a higher dimension, into a clearer spiritual light. Now I'm conscious about the truth in His words, when He stroked my arm and said, "We are one."

Sai Baba says that the divine atma, the life soul, is behind and in all life. "I am the sovereign atma, the soul, always present. I am not separate from God. I'm not different from you. You are all Avatars, but you are not conscious of your divinity." God is eternal. He is nothing distinct, he is the life in all.

God is the creator of our individual atma, our life soul, our conscious self, which from time to time enters a new body for a new life on Earth. This round goes on as long as we are bound to the cause and effect of the law of karma. As long as the illusion of our ego creates new karma we are reborn for a new period of learning and developing on Earth.

In India one inhales religion with every breath, the rhythm of life has a dominating element of religion, and the entire culture of India is marked thereby. Children grow up with religion as a natural part of everyday life. It is easy to understand why India is called a Holy Land. All religions are represented, all find their living space. In India God is worshipped by many names and with many forms, but behind all of them there is the same God, the one and only.

People from all over the world come to Sai Baba, all religions are represented around Him. Sai Baba says, "There is no reason for you to change the worship of your chosen God according to the religion you have grown up with and are used to. Your worship and your prayers reach the same God, who is behind all forms."

Each one talks about God on the basis of individual experience and belief. Many think of and describe God as a mystic spiritual being, incomprehensible to human beings. Since the beginning of time mankind has searched for God in both Heaven and on Earth. Had we but directed our search inward, within, we would have become conscious of His presence in our own heart.

We are entirely dependent on God, but God is not dependent on us. We live in an illusion that hides God's true nature, our own reality. We are all seekers, and each individual has to go his or her own way. Whichever way we choose, eventually it leads us home to God. We must show understanding and tolerance for those who follow another path. May every individual be allowed to worship God, extol His glory and majesty, in the way chosen as most appropriate. If we honestly, with longing and love, seek God, He will come to meet us on whatever path we have chosen to walk.

Truth is eternally the same, but my reality is, perhaps, not your reality. God is love and He exists for us all. Let us support and help each other in love on our pilgrimage through life.

To master our ego and our senses seems to be one of the most difficult things we have to learn. The temptation to follow the voice of the ego has led us farther and farther away from God. We have lost the ability to listen to Him in our inner being and instead have become more strongly bound to our ego and the illusory desires we create.

All religions have a common message: God is love, live in love. Mankind has failed miserably in realizing this divine message in life. History tells us in a frightening way how our interpretation of God's message has led to extreme disruption and innumerable religious wars all over the world, in all times. Even today we share this same experience. The question is inevitable and must be asked, "How can this happen and how can it go on in the same way in our more enlightened time? What is the reason for this ungodly, wicked behaviour?" And many keep asking, "Can there be God who allows this to be repeated generation after generation?" We make God responsible for our own misdeeds, but the truth is that we ourselves are responsible for our deeds.

We speak about God's message, that God is love, live in love - but we do the contrary. Tempted by our desire to possess power and position we forget both God and His teachings. We go away from God and create our own gods, who we worship and follow. These materialistic gods of the ego have made us blind to a true and righteous way of living. The individual in society fights to achieve personal favours, sordid gains and influence. This is like rings on the surface of water, which spread out increasingly wide and cannot be restrained. What began with a difference of opinions has ended in hatred and war. As long as we cannot live in love and peace and accept the divine oneness, conflict will continue to exist.

Our ego has created a dark, evil circle where we are imprisoned, and in our misfortune we crave that others shall submit to our belief, our pattern of life. When the pressure then becomes too strong for us to bear, the explosion brings about cruel actions and war. How shall we be able to lead others towards light, when we are blinded by the darkness of the ego and cannot even lead ourselves?

We worship and invoke God in shrines, but do not experience His love in our heart. Most often it only becomes a ceremonial experience, which does not leave any trace of light and love. We have turned away from God, but lament loudly that He no longer hears our prayers. We ourselves have created this separation from God. We have ourselves chosen, by so following the voice of the ego. If suffering and war are to cease on Earth, we must take the first step towards God and live in accordance with His message of love.

Love must stand at the centre of our life. We must learn to love, to fill our heart with love for God, for life, for all people irrespective of race and religion. We must free ourselves from the thought of dualism in our coexistence here on Earth. We are all brothers and sisters striving towards the same goal, to one day reach liberation from the cycle of rebirth. Sai Baba says, "Start the day with love, fill the day with love, end the day with love. That is the way to God."

Jesus announced, "What you do not wish others to do to you, that you should not do to them. Love also your enemies." We human beings must learn to understand the contents of Jesus' words, "I and the Father who sent me are the same. He who knows me, knows also the Father." Through this message we must understand that God the Father is not separate from us. We are all the same, we are all united in the oneness of the divine creation.

When we go away from God, we are no longer able to perceive His presence in our heart Our divine Self is covered by the veil of illusion. Therefore we identify ourselves with our body instead of with God, our soul, our real inner Self. We are so strongly bound to the I-consciousness of the body, that we cannot perceive God's light within. The world of illusion has become a substitute for reality. This takes us farther and farther away from God. As long as we do not have peace within and love in our heart the bonds of the ego will bind us to the suffering that our karma creates.

Through our actions we must show God that we seek and ask for His help. Then He will come to meet us and hear our prayers. Sai Baba says, "If you take one step towards me, I shall take ten steps towards you." God's grace is always there, but it must be reciprocated by our own efforts, to yield fruit.

We keep our outer appearance clean in order to make a good impression on others. We should also think about and make efforts to keep our heart pure, our heart where God lives and works.

If we want to change the world, stop wars and relieve distress on our Earth, we must change ourselves and live more selflessly, with compassionate love for each other. We cannot crave from society and others what we ourselves do not strive for and try to realize in our daily life. We have not only rights, but every right corresponds to an obligation toward our fellow-creatures. We must work to obliterate racial contradictions and religious intolerance. Our concern must be widened to enclose all human beings, irrespective of the country they live and work in. In this life time I live in Sweden, but my next life will, perhaps, be in another country, where individuals are oppressed and tortured. As we do not know where we may have to live in our future lives, we may ourselves be subjected to similar treatment to that we inflict on our brothers and sisters. Therefore it is important that we widen our view of life. We must learn to realize that our lives are connected with all living creatures, with all life. We are not separate individuals who can act at our own discretion and for our own pleasure, without others also being affected by our deeds.

If we but understood the meaning of the life principle of the divine creation, that we are one and forever connected with all life, we would not behave as we do in our ignorance and egoism. Only through enlightened awareness and a clearer consciousness can we learn to understand how important it is that we live in love beyond all limits. If we injure another, we unknowingly injure God. Since God pervades all we thus injure ourselves. We must be more humble, more tolerant and less selfish. We must become more enlightened and conscious, for only in this way can we save ourselves and the world from continued suffering. We must return to God and live in love with each other. God is love.

Let us humbly and wholeheartedly pray together and repeat the holy mantra:

Asato ma sad gamaya	From the unreal, lead us to the Real.
Tamaso ma jyotir gamaya	From darkness, lead us to Light.
Mrityor ma amritam gamaya	From death, lead us to Immortality.
OM Santhi, santhi, santhi.	OM. Peace, peace, peace.

Sai Ram

God Guides Us

For thousands of years saints, yogis, wise and pious men and women, have withdrawn from the world to develop their God-consciousness in stillness, to seek God within. Solitude and tranquillity they have found, for example, in the Himalayan mountains. Through their concentrated power of thought, which they sent out into the ether, they have created an aura which filled the air with spiritual light and energy. These places will be permeated by this aura in all future times. Those who visit these places can perceive this spiritual, divine atmosphere.

Invoking God in their prayers, the holy ones asked for His divine guidance to reach liberation from the wheel of rebirth. They sent forth healing, blessing vibrations, rays of light and love, for the good of the whole of humanity. The spiritual aspirant can experience God's obvious power in action at several places on Earth, but these perhaps, are not generally as well known as the Himalayas.

In the winter of 1986-87 I spent five months in Southern France, where I lived virtually isolated from people and the world, in stillness, on Mont des Roses, the Mount of Roses. The place where I rented a villa had once, long ago, been a monastery. I felt an atmosphere of spirituality and light, and was glad to live for several months in this divinely marked house. Here I lived close to nature and had daily walks in the beautiful surroundings. My days and nights were filled with peace and meditation, my thoughts were with God. During a walk, when I sat down on a boulder on top of the mountain, God gave me a wonderful, divine vision.

For several years I had meditated daily on the holy mantra AUM. This was also the case on this eventful day, and it was the introduction to the divine vision that followed. AUM resounded in my inner being. I was filled with light, and strong vibrations lifted my consciousness out of my body. Within I heard the echo of AUM, God's voice in the cosmos. On the bright rays of light I was carried further and further and was entirely enveloped by the divine cosmic light, in a colour spectrum of life and movement.

In this universal perspective the Earth was floating around its orbit in the cosmos, surrounded by brilliant light. A feeling of divine oneness filled me with bliss beyond words. I was carried further and further into the limitless cosmos. As in a divine dance I floated from one to the other of the innumerable planets of the universe. I was one with Brahman's universal creating soul and consciousness. I took the form of a flame and became part of the glowing substance of the sun.

I was a spiritual being who visited the various planets and solar systems in the cosmos. I was carried around and out into the endless universe, conscious that I had had innumerable existences and forms of divine life before my development on Earth as a human being had begun.

God! You are endless and infinite! And still You are one in the manifoldness of Your creation - all is God!

One day when my earthly pilgrimage is over my soul will return and merge in its cosmic source.

As quietly as my consciousness had left my body on the rays of light, as quietly I was brought back from this divine vision and journey in the cosmos. Without the grace of God I would not have experienced this fascinating cosmic vision nor been able to preserve the memory.

In my search for Truth, the Truth of God's reality, God has given me the answers to my questions, "Who am I? From where do I come and where am I going?" Sai Baba, who knew my longing and love for God, enlightened my mind, so that the light of the soul could spread itself in my inner being and make me conscious of my true Self and the oneness of the divine cosmic creation.

Few are those who try, and still less those who succeed in understanding the meaning of life. If we are not conscious about our inner reality, how can we understand God's true nature, His reality in the universal creation? When we have freed ourselves from our illusory I-consciousness we recognize our divine inner Self, God, our true nature. We must struggle through earthly life after earthly life until we have freed ourselves from the illusion of duality and become conscious of God's true reality. Not until then can we understand that we are Gods who have taken human form.

God remains always the same. He reveals Himself to us in love, for He is love. He reveals Himself to us in light, for He is light. He reveals Himself to us in life, for He is life. God is our soul, atma, the only reality.

After my first meeting with Sai Baba, whenever I prayed and called for Him, His presence has been as vibrant for me as when I was sitting at His divine Lotus Feet in Prasanthi Nilayam, even when I was thousands of miles away from His physical presence. God's true being is not bound to a certain place on Earth. God's spirit and power is omnipresent in the whole of the endless universe.

Four times Sisko and I have visited Sai Baba in India, adding up to a period of about one year. We were happy to live in His divine nearness, a divine grace and privilege which has made a deep impact on our spiritual development and our daily life. Perhaps once more in the future we shall experience that privilege to stay near Him and feel His divine radiation of love and peace.

In my heart I feel deep love and humble gratitude to Sai Baba for all He in His divine grace has given me - limitless love, inspiration, strength and guidance, understanding and forgiveness. With divine patience He has spread light on my path and lifted me up from the darkness of ignorance into a clearer, purer consciousness.

Many times I have asked myself how I, even to a small extent, shall be able to reciprocate His divine blessings. Sai Baba Himself has given me the answer: only through selfless love and service to God in all beings and through all actions, by spreading love and light without limits and expectations, to His glory, in His name.

Oh Lord
Lead us. Liberate us from the bonds of illusion.
Let us become conscious of Your divine glory in all
appearances of life.
Let us perceive Your light within.
Let Your love reveal itself in our heart and guide our
thoughts and deeds.
Let Your perfection appear in our life.
Let Your divine wisdom reveal itself in our consciousness
so that we can understand that You
are the only true divine power working in us.
Let us see the good, see the light in our fellow-beings.
Let us be Your light, shining in the darkness.
Dear Sai Baba
In humble gratitude I bend down to Your divine Lotus
Feet and ask You to accept my love.

Sai Ram.

I wish to conclude by sharing with the reader a poem written by a true Sai-devotee, my wife Sisko.

A Prayer of Love

Oh God
Give me love
Let me love with all Your power.

Please
Let Your love flow through me
Flow freely, generously, joyfully
Without limits, without reason
Without expectation
Flow to Your glory
Flow from You
To You in all.

Please
Give my love power
To reach all
To embrace all
To conquer every obstacle.

Give my love patience to endure all
Courage to suffer and sacrifice all
Courage and strength to see the truth
Humility to understand and forgive all.

Please
Let Your love
Transform hate and jealousy into love
Greed and selfishness into giving and offering.

Please
Let Your love through me
Bring light into darkness
Warmth into cold
Let it bring freedom to the oppressed
Joy to the sorrowful
And strength to the weak.

Let Your love
Bring rest and encouragement to the tired
Inspiration, hope and faith to the disappointed
Let it still the deep pain of yearning
The agitations of the mind.

Please
Let Your love show the way home for the homeless and the lost
Dry the tears of loneliness
Bring peace into crying hearts
Let it take me beyond the horizon of earthly struggle
Take me to the glorious dawn of divinity.

Only Your love
Can lead me
To full consciousness of Your reality
Your love in me
My love for You
In all and everything.

Oh Lord
I thank You
For Your mercy
For Your love
Forever.

Our beloved Lord Sai Baba -
You are life.
You are love.

Light spreads; it mingles with the light from other sources of light; it has no boundaries, no prejudices, no favourites. You may not like your neighbour, but the light from the lamp on your verandah shines hand in hand with the lamp on his verandah. You cannot keep it back!

Learn this lesson of light and love; move out, clasp, spread, expand, give up limits of mine and thine, his and theirs, caste and creed in one limitless flow of Love. That is the culmination of all spiritual endeavour.

All the religions demand that their followers be good, see good and do good. No religion approves untruth and injustice. Thus, in essence, they are all one and have a common goal, while in details they may differ and follow different paths to reach the same goal. Let the different faiths flourish. Let the glory of God be sung in all the languages, in a variety of tunes. That should be the ideal. Respect the differences between the faiths and recognise them as valid so long as they do not extinguish the flame of Unity.

God is one and only one without equal, but known to people in diverse forms and names. Form and name are transient and change with time. The unchanging truth, beauty and love continue to hold the devotion of the followers of all religions.

See this unity in all living creatures, serve them with love and selflessness, banish your ego and pride and realise God's omnipresence. Just as there is only one Sun which is reflected in a million tanks, wells and ponds, there is only one God whose reflection can be seen in all creation.

There is only **one religion**, the **religion of Love**
There is only **one language**, the **language of the heart**
There is only **one caste**, the **caste of humanity**
There is only **one law**, the **law of work (duty)**
There is only **one God** and **He is Omnipresent**

Sai Baba, Quoted from Bangalore Newspaper, 1992

The Sathya Sai Symbol (as displayed in India)
And Its Significance*

"Listen to the primeval Pranava AUM resounding in your heart as well as the heart of the Universe"

"Remember the Wheel of Cause and Consequence, of Deed and Destiny and the Wheel of Dharma that rights them all"

"Offer all bitterness in the sacred Fire and emerge grand, great and Godly"

"Be like the Star which never wavers from the Crescent but is fixed in steady faith"

"Cut the 'I' feeling clean across and let your ego die on the Cross, to endow on you Eternity"

The Sai Insignia exemplifies the unity of all religions

* The above 5 symbols were chosen by Sai Baba as they were representative of mainstream religions in India. Some countries outside of India have added other religious symbols as suitable to their areas.